NEW DIRECTIONS FOR EVALUATION
A PUBLICATION OF THE AMERICAN EVALUATION ASSOCIATION

Gary T. Henry, *Georgia State University*
COEDITOR-IN-CHIEF

Jennifer C. Greene, *University of Illinois*
COEDITOR-IN-CHIEF

Using Appreciative Inquiry in Evaluation

Hallie Preskill
University of New Mexico

Anne T. Coghlan
ATC Consulting

EDITORS

Number 100, Winter 2003

JOSSEY-BASS
San Francisco

USING APPRECIATIVE INQUIRY IN EVALUATION
Hallie Preskill, Anne T. Coghlan (eds.)
New Directions for Evaluation, no. 100
Jennifer C. Greene, Gary T. Henry, Coeditors-in-Chief
Copyright ©2003 Wiley Periodicals, Inc., A Wiley company

Microfilm copies of issues and articles are available in 16mm and 35mm, as well as microfiche in 105mm, through University Microfilms Inc., 300 North Zeeb Road, Ann Arbor, Michigan 48106-1346.

New Directions for Evaluation is indexed in Contents Pages in Education, Higher Education Abstracts, and Sociological Abstracts.

Print ISSN: 1097-6736; Online ISSN: 1534-875X

NEW DIRECTIONS FOR EVALUATION is part of The Jossey-Bass Education Series and is published quarterly by Wiley Subscription Services, Inc., a Wiley company, at Jossey-Bass, 989 Market Street, San Francisco, California 94103-1741.

SUBSCRIPTIONS cost $80.00 for U.S./Canada/Mexico; $104 international. For institutions, agencies, and libraries, $175 U.S.; $215 Canada; $249 international. Prices subject to change.

EDITORIAL CORRESPONDENCE should be addressed to the Editors-in-Chief, Jennifer C. Greene, Department of Educational Psychology, University of Illinois, 260E Education Building, 1310 South Sixth Street, Champaign, IL 61820, or Gary T. Henry, School of Policy Studies, Georgia State University, P.O. Box 4039, Atlanta, GA 30302-4039.

www.josseybass.com

Editorial Policy and Procedures

New Directions for Evaluation, a quarterly sourcebook, is an official publication of the American Evaluation Association. The journal publishes empirical, methodological, and theoretical works on all aspects of evaluation. A reflective approach to evaluation is an essential strand to be woven through every volume. The editors encourage volumes that have one of three foci: (1) craft volumes that present approaches, methods, or techniques that can be applied in evaluation practice, such as the use of templates, case studies, or survey research; (2) professional issue volumes that present issues of import for the field of evaluation, such as utilization of evaluation or locus of evaluation capacity; (3) societal issue volumes that draw out the implications of intellectual, social, or cultural developments for the field of evaluation, such as the women's movement, communitarianism, or multiculturalism. A wide range of substantive domains is appropriate for *New Directions for Evaluation;* however, the domains must be of interest to a large audience within the field of evaluation. We encourage a diversity of perspectives and experiences within each volume, as well as creative bridges between evaluation and other sectors of our collective lives.

The editors do not consider or publish unsolicited single manuscripts. Each issue of the journal is devoted to a single topic, with contributions solicited, organized, reviewed, and edited by a guest editor. Issues may take any of several forms, such as a series of related chapters, a debate, or a long article followed by brief critical commentaries. In all cases, the proposals must follow a specific format, which can be obtained from the editor-in-chief. These proposals are sent to members of the editorial board and to relevant substantive experts for peer review. The process may result in acceptance, a recommendation to revise and resubmit, or rejection. However, the editors are committed to working constructively with potential guest editors to help them develop acceptable proposals.

Jennifer C. Greene, Coeditor-in-Chief
Department of Educational Psychology
University of Illinois
260E Education Building
1310 South Sixth Street
Champaign, IL 61820
e-mail: jcgreene@uiuc.edu

Gary T. Henry, Coeditor-in-Chief
School of Policy Studies
Georgia State University
P.O. Box 4039
Atlanta, GA 30302-4039
e-mail: gthenry@gsu.edu

SERIES EDITORS' NOTES

New Directions for Evaluation crosses a milestone with this volume: volume 100. Initiated twenty-five years ago as a thematic journal to fill a void in the publishing field, it is now in the good company of many other evaluation-oriented journals, but it maintains its unique thematic character. We have served as editors for over eight years and have been privileged to have edited over a quarter of the volumes. We framed our editorship with a number of goals: to have all chapters in a volume closely linked to the theme, to combine caution or dissent in every volume that enthusiastically described a new direction, to attract the interest of every member of the American Evaluation Association in at least two of the four volumes in a year, and to present new directions in both thought and practice. At times we struggled to fulfill these ideals. We struggled with uneven flows of proposals, getting timely reviews, meeting deadlines, waiting in vain for proposals that should have been, locating newcomers with unproven but creative and exciting ideas, and choosing between providing encouragement and allowing folks to cut their losses.

Yet in the appreciative spirit of this volume, we have much to appreciate: Lois-ellin Datta for her exemplary guidance and leadership during our apprenticeship as associate editors, the dedicated members of our advisory board who supported our editorship with thoughtful and critically helpful proposal reviews, each other for a collegial respect that readily crossed boundaries of methodological tradition and temperament, and especially the many members of the evaluation community who did the substantive work of this journal, taking the time to share their evaluation practices, ideas, reflections, and enthusiasm with others in our community.

We now turn the editing work over to very capable hands: editor-in-chief Jean King and her associate editors, Robin Miller and Nancy Zajano. We very much appreciate their willingness to assume these responsibilities, and we look forward to appreciating their vision of new directions in evaluation.

Gary T. Henry
Jennifer C. Greene
Coeditors-in-Chief

CONTENTS

EDITORS' NOTES

When people ask us why we are evaluators and why we do this work, a common response is our desire to assist organizations and programs to be more effective. We are always searching for ways to make evaluations more useful and meaningful to stakeholders. To this end, each of us has incorporated stakeholder, participatory, and learning-oriented approaches into our work. Nevertheless, we still struggle with stakeholders' negative perceptions of evaluation, the apathy often associated with problem-solving efforts, and stakeholders' difficulty in using the findings once the evaluators have finished their work. In the past few years, however, we have both experienced the excitement and creative energy that Appreciative Inquiry generates among our project stakeholders. As a result, we began to wonder if there was a place for Appreciative Inquiry in the evaluator's toolbox. After many conversations about the possibilities of using Appreciative Inquiry in evaluation practice, we decided it was time to introduce it to the field of evaluation and to explore why, when, and how it might be used in evaluative inquiry.

Appreciative Inquiry is a process that searches for what is best in people and organizations. It is a participative, collaborative, and systematic approach to inquiry that seeks what is right in an organization in order to create a desired future. Ultimately, it is a process and a method for asking questions designed to strengthen a system's capacity for organizational learning and creativity. Appreciative Inquiry's focus on identifying what is best and most successful as a means for moving forward made us think about how often evaluation is construed as a means for identifying concerns, issues, and problems in order to develop solutions. As such, the language of evaluation is often deficit based. Although evaluators certainly strive to find what is working well, they also focus heavily on searching for what is wrong and what is not working, often concluding their work with a list of recommendations to improve the evaluand. These problem-seeking intentions are not always evident in the evaluation's guiding questions, but they often are operationalized in survey and interview questions asked of participants. For example, evaluators might ask respondents to identify barriers or challenges to their work, discuss why things do not seem to be effective, or explain why a certain expected outcome was not achieved. Appreciative Inquiry, in contrast, shifts the language used to a more positive, affirmative stance. In doing this, participants and respondents identify what has been successful; from these successes, they can then create a future filled with more of these successes. As a result, problems and issues are still addressed as they are in conventional evaluation, but in a very different way.

NEW DIRECTIONS FOR EVALUATION, no. 100, Winter 2003 © Wiley Periodicals, Inc.

As the chapters in this volume illustrate, Appreciative Inquiry offers evaluators an approach and method for discovering and building on the positive aspects of a program (or any evaluand). The chapters explore the following questions:

- What is the potential role of Appreciative Inquiry in evaluation?
- In what ways does Appreciative Inquiry constitute an overall approach to evaluation? In what ways is it better construed as a data collection method?
- What impact does using Appreciative Inquiry in evaluation have on the use of evaluation processes and findings?
- What contextual factors or conditions make the use of Appreciative Inquiry in evaluation appropriate?
- What are the challenges in using Appreciative Inquiry in evaluation?
- To what extent and how does Appreciative Inquiry in evaluation address program issues and problems if its focus is on what is working well?
- What are the areas or issues that need further research regarding the use of Appreciative Inquiry in evaluation work?

Chapter One, which we wrote with Tessie Tzavaras Catsambas, describes the philosophy, assumptions, and processes of Appreciative Inquiry and how it fits within the landscape of evaluation practice. It also provides the framework and language for Chapters Two through Five, which are case studies of situations in which Appreciative Inquiry was used to conduct various kinds of evaluation studies. Because the use of Appreciative Inquiry in evaluation poses a number of interesting questions and challenges, Patricia Rogers and Dugan Fraser (in Chapter Six) and Michael Quinn Patton (in Chapter Seven) critique the use of Appreciative Inquiry in evaluation.

We invited individuals to submit abstracts describing how they have used Appreciative Inquiry in their evaluation work, and from these we selected four cases based on certain criteria, including the author's knowledge of evaluation and Appreciative Inquiry, the questions raised about the opportunities and challenges related to integrating Appreciative Inquiry and evaluation, and the type of program and context represented. To ensure that the critical issues regarding Appreciative Inquiry and its use in evaluation were addressed, we asked each of the authors to cover the following issues when writing their case:

- Background to and a description of the evaluation, including what was evaluated, what the overall purpose of the evaluation was, and what the key evaluation questions were
- Evaluation design and data collection methods, including why Appreciative Inquiry was chosen for the evaluation and how it was used
- Evaluation findings and the benefits of using Appreciative Inquiry to obtain these findings

- Issues in using Appreciative Inquiry in evaluation, specifically how problems or program weaknesses were dealt with during the evaluation

The case study chapters represent various applications of Appreciative Inquiry in a wide range of contexts. An evaluation of an academic department in a private secondary school is the focus of Chapter Two. Sheila McNamee describes how she used all four Appreciative Inquiry phases to assess the department's curriculum with a staff that had assumed oppositional positions with regard to the school's curriculum. She describes in detail how using Appreciative Inquiry not only changed how the staff relate to one another, but also diminished the significance of their perceived differences. As a result, in addition to providing valuable and useful information, Appreciative Inquiry transformed the ways in which the staff members work together. Because the author's approach encompassed both evaluation and organizational development practices, it is an example of how the lines between evaluation and organizational development can become blurred when using Appreciative Inquiry. In Chapter Seven, Patton addresses the extent to which this is a problem and whether this is inevitable.

Chapter Three explores an evaluation of the African Women's Media Center in which Tessie Tzavaras Catsambas and Laverne Webb used Appreciative Inquiry processes to develop the evaluation's focus and key questions, as well as to design and implement several data collection methods. In addition to describing some of the findings from these methods, the authors discuss how using Appreciative Inquiry revealed specific controversial issues that the organization later resolved. They also explore some of the challenges they faced in conducting this and similar evaluations, including how they address problems when using Appreciative Inquiry, the limitations of Appreciative Inquiry, and the challenges of staying within an appreciative framework and the original scope of the evaluation.

The focus of Chapter Four is an evaluation of the program of the Family Rehabilitation Center, a nongovernmental, humanitarian, nonprofit service organization in Sri Lanka. The program's long-term objective is to reduce the practice of torture and meet the medical and psychological needs of victims of torture and trauma throughout the country. Mette Jacobsgaard describes how Appreciative Inquiry was chosen as an evaluation approach when it became clear that previous evaluations had left the staff fearful, angry, and disillusioned. She explains how using two of the Appreciative Inquiry phases helped the staff uncover examples and stories of how they were indeed meeting the funder's requirements and were achieving their short-term objectives, a finding that was not present in earlier evaluation studies.

In Chapter Five, Dawn Hanson Smart and Mariann Mann describe an evaluation of the Girl Scouts Beyond Bars program that incorporated appreciatively oriented questions in focus group interviews and a survey, which were used in conjunction with more conventional evaluation methods.

This case illustrates how evaluators may use only one phase of the Appreciative Inquiry process in order to obtain a better understanding of what is most meaningful about a program and to identify ways to build on the best there is.

In Chapter Six, Patricia Rogers and Dugan Fraser offer a critical look at Appreciative Inquiry, particularly in reference to the cases presented in the chapters. They write that Appreciative Inquiry can be a useful and valuable technique in certain situations, but express concerns about applying it for the wrong reasons and with evaluators who might not have the group process and facilitation skills Appreciative Inquiry requires. Although they believe the cases reported here are interesting and instructive of how Appreciative Inquiry can be applied within an evaluation context, they suggest that the cases could have provided more guidance for evaluators on how to implement Appreciative Inquiry and more cautions about the dangers of using Appreciative Inquiry inappropriately.

Finally, in Chapter Seven, Michael Quinn Patton reflects on the origins of Appreciative Inquiry and its relationship to various evaluation purposes and approaches. He discusses evaluation definitions, the power of language, the importance of using Appreciative Inquiry in the right situations, and how Appreciative Inquiry relates to utilization-focused evaluation. He suggests that Appreciative Inquiry offers evaluators a valuable approach to evaluative inquiry and that we should continue to study its uses and effects.

One of the reasons we wanted to put this volume together is that we knew we would learn a great deal from the chapter authors. We have not been disappointed. From hearing their stories, we have become increasingly confident that Appreciative Inquiry has a place in the evaluator's toolkit. At the same time, we remind readers that this volume on Appreciative Inquiry and evaluation is only the beginning of an exploration that we hope will be stimulating, provocative, and ultimately helpful to evaluation practitioners and researchers. We welcome any and all thoughts, reactions, and ideas to further this conversation and exploration.

Hallie Preskill
Anne T. Coghlan
Editors

HALLIE PRESKILL is professor of organizational learning and instructional technologies at the University of New Mexico.

ANNE T. COGHLAN is an independent evaluation consultant based in Dhaka, Bangladesh.

Appreciative inquiry is an approach to seeking what is right in an organization in order to create a better future for it. How and when it might be used in evaluation practice is explored in this chapter.

An Overview of Appreciative Inquiry in Evaluation

Anne T. Coghlan, Hallie Preskill, Tessie Tzavaras Catsambas

Appreciative Inquiry is a relatively new asset-based approach from the field of organizational development that has been garnering attention for its successful application in facilitating organizational change. Appreciative Inquiry is a process that inquires into, identifies, and further develops the best of what is in organizations in order to create a better future. A fundamental premise is that "organizations move toward what they study" (Cooperrider, Whitney, and Stavros, 2003, p. 29).

A wide range of approaches, including Total Quality Management, Continuous Quality Improvement, the Balanced Score Card, Future Search, Open Space, and Appreciative Inquiry, have led change management efforts. The strategies outlined in these approaches vary; they include, among others, using measurement and evidence-based decisions for quality improvement, employing mediation and negotiation for the discovery of common ground, and following processes that aim to build organizational assets. While organizational development methods differ greatly depending on the purpose of the intervention and the organization's population and context, many approaches tend to focus on identifying specific problems, analyzing possible causes and solutions to these problems, and devising a plan to resolve or eliminate the problems.

Appreciative Inquiry looks at organizational issues, challenges, and concerns in a significantly different way. Instead of focusing on problems, organizational members first discover what is working particularly well in their organization. Then, instead of analyzing possible causes and solutions, they envision what it might be like if "the best of what is" occurred more frequently. Here participants engage in a dialogue concerning what is needed, in terms of both tasks and resources, to bring about the desired future. Finally, organization members implement their desired changes. A common underlying assumption of problem-solving approaches is that organizations are served best by identifying and removing their deficits. In contrast, Appreciative Inquiry argues that organizations improve more effectively through "discovery and valuing, envisioning, dialogue and co-constructing the future" (Ashford and Patkar, 2001, p. 4).

The power of Appreciative Inquiry is the way in which participants become engaged and inspired by focusing on their own positive experiences. Usually in a workshop setting, participants remember and relate personal experiences of success, identify the common elements of these experiences, and devise statements and action plans for making those experiences occur more often in the organization. Because Appreciative Inquiry focuses on the positive and is grounded in participants' actual experiences, they "walk away with a sense of commitment, confidence and affirmation that they have been successful. They also know clearly how to make more moments of success" (Hammond, 1996, p. 7).

According to its proponents, Appreciative Inquiry is not just another organizational development tool or technique but "a philosophy and orientation to change that can fundamentally reshape the practice of organizational learning, design and development" (Watkins and Mohr, 2001, p. 21). It is an alternative approach, framework, or mind-set that focuses on illuminating and affirming personal success factors or forces within an organization to use with existing organizational development interventions such as strategic planning, organizational design or restructuring, and project evaluations (Watkins and Mohr, 2001). As such, it is both a philosophy and a worldview, with particular principles and assumptions and a structured set of core processes and practices for engaging people in identifying and cocreating an organization's future.

A common criticism of Appreciative Inquiry is that it ignores or even denies problems. While at first blush this view may seem understandable, it is nevertheless untrue. Appreciative Inquiry does address issues and problems, but from a different and often more constructive perspective: it reframes problem statements into a focus on strengths and successes. For example, rather than ask participants to list the problems their organization is facing, they are asked to explain what is going well, why it is going well, and what they want more of in the organization. In some Appreciative Inquiry efforts, participants are also asked to state their specific wishes for the organization. This implicitly raises and addresses problems. "More broadly, Appreciative Inquiry does not turn a blind eye on 'negative' situations or 'deficit-oriented' realities in organizations; it does not substitute a 'rosy' and 'romantic' picture for an 'objective' and 'realistic' one. It accepts these realities for what they are—areas in need of conversations and transformation. . . . But [Appreciative Inquiry] intentionally shifts the focus of the inquiry and intervention to those realities that are sources of vitality"

(Banaga, 1998, p. 263). Whitney and Trosten-Bloom (2003) add, "We do not dismiss accounts of conflict, problems, or stress. We simply do not use them as the basis of analysis or action" (p. 18).

Perhaps the best explanation for the benefits of Appreciative Inquiry is from Tom White, former president of GTE Telephone Operations, shortly after completing an Appreciative Inquiry process:

> Appreciative Inquiry can get you much better results than seeking out and solving problems. . . . If you combine a negative culture with all the challenges we face today, it could be easy to convince ourselves that we have too many problems to overcome—to slip into a paralyzing sense of helplessness. . . . Don't get me wrong. I'm not advocating mindless happy talk. Appreciative Inquiry is a complex science designed to make things better. We can't ignore problems—we just need to approach them from the other side [Cooperrider and Whitney, 2000, p. 7].

History of Appreciative Inquiry

Appreciative Inquiry is based on the work of David Cooperrider, who in 1980 as a doctoral student at Case Western Reserve University intended to study physician leadership in one of the most highly regarded medical centers in the United States. After asking physician leaders to tell their stories of successes and failures, he was amazed at the level of positive cooperation, innovation, and egalitarian governance when they were most effective. As a result of this finding, he decided to look at only those data that described the physician's leadership and the organization when it was most effective: when it was at its best. "The results of the study created such a powerful positive stir that the board requested this [Appreciative Inquiry] method be used at all levels of the 8000-person organization to facilitate change" (Cooperrider, Whitney, and Stavros, 2003, p. xxiv).

Over the past two decades, Appreciative Inquiry has evolved from what began as an academic theory-building effort to a practical and powerful process for organizations to learn about and transform their processes and systems. Since the mid-1980s, the practice of Appreciative Inquiry has been applied in diverse settings in the United States and internationally. Numerous articles and books documenting its theory and application have been published, and Appreciative Inquiry-focused workshops and conferences have been offered throughout the world. Over the years, the theory and practice of Appreciative Inquiry has evolved into a comprehensive organizational intervention framework. A number of milestones mark its development (Watkins and Mohr, 2001):

• In 1990, the Taos Institute was founded by several Appreciative Inquiry practitioners and became a world-renowned training center for organizations, consultants, family therapists, educators, and others.

• In 1990, the Global Excellence in Management Initiative was begun with funding by the U.S. Agency for International Development to promote organizational excellence in development organizations in the United States and abroad. The initiative fostered innovative uses of Appreciative Inquiry in the international development field and created strong Appreciative Inquiry groups in Africa, Asia, and Latin America.

• In 1992, Imagine Chicago was started as a large-scale community development effort in which children conducted hundreds of appreciative interviews with adults and elders throughout the city. This highly successful effort generated additional "Imagine" projects in other countries, including Australia and India, and in several other U.S. cities and states.

• In the mid-1990s, an Appreciative Inquiry-based international conference took place that offered participants an opportunity to build partnerships between corporations, foundations, nongovernment organizations, and governments across countries. In addition, the United Religions Initiative started using Appreciative Inquiry to bring together the world's religions in support of peace. Later, David Cooperrider was asked to bring Appreciative Inquiry into a world peace program started by the Dalai Lama.

• By 2000, in addition to the publication of books and articles, other means of disseminating information about Appreciative Inquiry were established, including annual conferences, an electronic newsletter, a listserv (ailist@lists.business.utah.edu), and several regional Appreciative Inquiry networks.

The overall impact of Appreciative Inquiry on the organizational development field has been significant. This impact was predicted and summarized by Richard Beckhard, one of the founders of the profession in his presentation to the National Academy of Management Conference in August 1999: "Appreciative Inquiry is, in my view, an exciting breakthrough, one that signals a change in the way we think about change. I'm intrigued by how rapidly it is emerging; but it is something substantive, conceptually strong, not like the quick fads. In my view we are looking at something important—[Appreciative Inquiry] will be of enduring consequence and energizing innovation for the field" (Watkins and Mohr, 2001, p. xxv).

Core Principles and Assumptions of Appreciative Inquiry

As the practice of Appreciative Inquiry has evolved, so have its core principles, assumptions, and processes. Ken Gergen's book, *Toward Transformation in Social Knowledge* (1994, 1982), and the theory of social constructionism have strongly influenced the development of Appreciative Inquiry. Social constructionism reflects a belief that there is no one reality or truth; rather, truth is grounded in the multiple and contextually determined realities of individuals' perceptions, dialogues, and shared understandings.

In developing Appreciative Inquiry, Cooperrider was also influenced by numerous research studies from the fields of medicine, sports, behavioral sciences, and anthropology that demonstrated the power of positive images. The first such finding was the placebo effect, in which one- to two-thirds of patients showed marked improvement in symptoms by believing they had received effective treatment. A second set of influential findings was from the Pygmalion studies, which demonstrated the relationship between the images teachers have of their students and the students' levels of performance and long-term futures. A third set of studies showed the effects of both positive and negative thinking on the outcomes of surgery: patients with more positive thoughts recovered at a much faster rate (Cooperrider and Whitney, 2000).

Cooperrider and others applied the theories of social constructionism and the power of image to organizational change and developed the following five core principles for the practice of Appreciative Inquiry (Cooperrider and Whitney, 2000):

1. *Constructivist Principle.* Related to the notion that multiple realities exist based on perceptions and shared understandings, this principle suggests that what is known about an organization and the organization's actual destiny are interwoven.

2. *Principle of Simultaneity:* Because reality is an evolving social construction, it is possible through inquiry to influence the reality an organization creates for itself. Inquiry and change are simultaneous and "inquiry is intervention." Thus, the nature of the inquiry itself is critically important where the very first questions we ask set the stage for what people discover and learn and the way they coconstruct their future.

3. *Poetic Principle.* Because reality is a human construction, an organization is like an open book in which its story is being coauthored continually by its members and those who interact with them. Consequently, members are free to choose which part of the story to study or inquire about—its problems and needs, or its moments of creativity or joy, or both.

4. *Anticipatory Principle.* This principle postulates that the image an organization has of its future guides that organization's current behavior. Thus, an organization's positive images of its future will anticipate, or lead to, positive actions.

5. *Positive Principle.* This principle arose from extensive experience with Appreciative Inquiry. Early Appreciative Inquiry practitioners found that the more positive the questions they asked were, the more engaged and excited participants were and the more successful and longer lasting the change effort was. This is in large part because human beings and organizations want to turn toward positive images that give them energy and nourish happiness.

Based on these principles, eight assumptions form the foundation for Appreciative Inquiry's processes and methods (Hammond, 1996, pp. 20–21):

1. In every society, organization, or group, something works.
2. What we focus on becomes our reality.
3. Reality is created in the moment, and there are multiple realities.
4. The act of asking questions of an organization or group influences the group in some way.
5. People have more confidence and comfort to journey to the future (the unknown) when they carry forward parts of the past (the known).
6. If we carry parts of the past forward, they should be what is best about the past.
7. It is important to value differences.
8. The language we use creates our reality.

These principles and assumptions underlie both the philosophy of Appreciative Inquiry and the ways in which it is conducted.

Appreciative Inquiry Models, Processes, and Methods

Of the two primary models for conducting Appreciative Inquiry, the more common is the 4-D model (Figure 1.1). The first phase in the model, Discovery, consists of participants interviewing each other and sharing stories about their peak experiences. The following foundational (or generic) questions guide these interviews (Cooperrider, Whitney, and Stavros, 2003, p. 23):

- Describe a high-point experience in your organization—a time when you were most alive and engaged.
- Without being modest, what is it that you most value about yourself, your work, and your organization?
- What are the core factors that give life to your organization, without which the organization would cease to exist?
- What three wishes do you have to enhance the health and vitality of your organization?

Participants share their individual stories in pairs and then with the larger group, and together they identify key topics or themes common to the stories. They then create a customized interview protocol by selecting three to five of the identified topics or themes and writing several appreciative questions for each. Using the new protocol, interviews are conducted with as many organization members as possible, ideally by the members themselves.

Participants then begin the Dream phase: based on the information obtained from the interviews, they envision themselves and their organization functioning at their best. Through various kinds of visualization and other creative exercises, participants think broadly and holistically about a desirable future. Based on these dreams, and in the Design phase,

Figure 1.1. Appreciative Inquiry 4-D Model

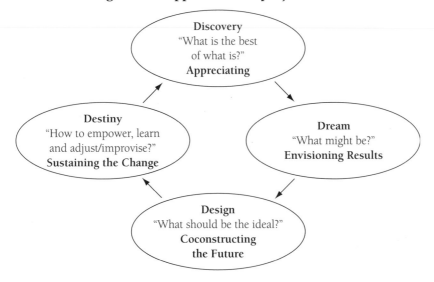

Source: Adapted from Watkins and Mohr (2001).

participants propose strategies, processes, and systems; make decisions; and develop collaborations that will create and support positive change. They develop provocative propositions or possibility and design statements that are concrete, detailed visions based on what was discovered about past successes. In the Destiny phase, participants begin to implement both their overall visions of the Dream phase and the specific provocative propositions of the Design stage. This phase is ongoing as participants continue to implement changes, monitor their progress, and engage in new dialogue and Appreciative Inquiries.

A slightly different model illustrating Appreciative Inquiry processes is the 4-I model (Figure 1.2), developed by Mohr and Jacobsgaard (Watkins and Mohr, 2001). Its phases are Initiate, Inquire, Imagine, and Innovate.

The models, which are similar, have two major differences: (1) they use different language to describe the various phases, and (2) they present a different delineation of the phases. The 4-D model has a Destiny or Deliver phase that relates to implementation, while the 4-I model has an extra early planning step, Initiate, and embeds implementation into the Innovate phase. These subtle differences, along with those found in some of the case studies presented in the following chapters, have evolved based on the facilitators' experiences implementing Appreciative Inquiry with different audiences and in varying contexts. This continuous adaptation is an illustration of the dynamic nature of Appreciative Inquiry and its models and applications. Regardless of the model used, neither prescribes a rigid process. For example, when Appreciative Inquiry is implemented in real-world

Figure 1.2. Appreciative Inquiry 4-I Model

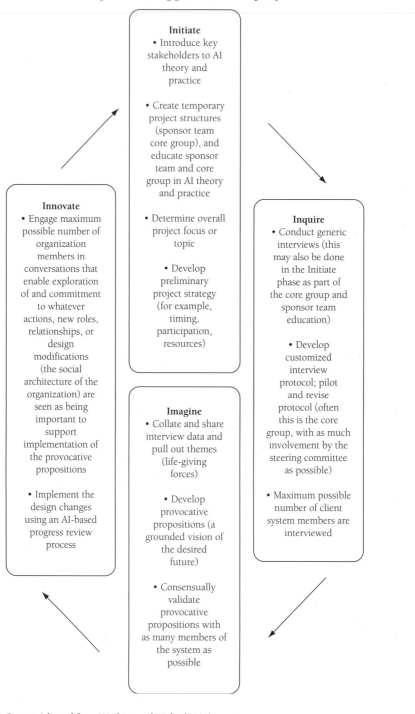

Initiate
- Introduce key stakeholders to AI theory and practice

- Create temporary project structures (sponsor team core group), and educate sponsor team and core group in AI theory and practice

- Determine overall project focus or topic

- Develop preliminary project strategy (for example, timing, participation, resources)

Innovate
- Engage maximum possible number of organization members in conversations that enable exploration of and commitment to whatever actions, new roles, relationships, or design modifications (the social architecture of the organization) are seen as being important to support implementation of the provocative propositions

- Implement the design changes using an AI-based progress review process

Inquire
- Conduct generic interviews (this may also be done in the Initiate phase as part of the core group and sponsor team education)

- Develop customized interview protocol; pilot and revise protocol (often this is the core group, with as much involvement by the steering committee as possible)

- Maximum possible number of client system members are interviewed

Imagine
- Collate and share interview data and pull out themes (life-giving forces)

- Develop provocative propositions (a grounded vision of the desired future)

- Consensually validate provocative propositions with as many members of the system as possible

Source: Adapted from Watkins and Mohr (2001).

settings, the various phases often overlap and repeat themselves in unpredictable ways, and some steps may fall into various stages.

Clearly, each Appreciative Inquiry effort needs to be adapted to the context in which it is being conducted and to the topic of the inquiry. The application of Appreciative Inquiry to evaluation is an example of one type of adaptation. Later in this chapter, we share some examples of how Appreciative Inquiry has been used in an evaluation context. First, however, we provide examples of where it has been used within an organizational development context using both the 4-D and 4-I models (L. Webb, personal communication, Apr. 3, 2003).

Catholic Relief Services (CRS). This sixty-year-old international development organization revitalized its relationships with local partner agencies through an Appreciative Inquiry process that over two and a half years brought field offices into dialogue and reflection with its partners in southern Africa, Eastern Europe, and South Asia about just and quality partnerships. CRS works entirely through partners such as local Catholic churches and compatible nongovernmental organizations. To model such relationships, it formed a partnership with the GEM Initiative (Global Excellence in Management) of Case Western Reserve University to guide this work.

CRS followed the 4-D cycle, holding two global partnership meetings and then coaching pilot countries to use appreciative interviews to discover what gives life to their partnerships through examples of past successes and resolving and reconciling past misunderstandings. They then dreamed about the effective and excellent partnerships they wanted to create together. The data from the partnership meetings fed into an international partnership conference in 2000. In a three-day conference, CRS and partners designed systems, policies, and procedures to make them more congruent with their emerging vision of partnership principles. The data from the partnership meetings fed into two international partnership summits in 1998 and 2000. This strategic process eventually contributed significantly to a 2001 World Summit that developed the agency's vision for the next ten years and involved four thousand staff in eighty countries. Also as part of the delivery phase, CRS has launched the implementation of the vision. According to Meg Kinghorn, CRS's technical adviser for partnership and capacity building at that time, relationships changed as soon as people started talking about what they had jointly achieved and what was really important in working together (C. Liebler, personal communication, Mar. 30, 2003). GEM codirector Claudia Liebler stated, "We did make an impact—we created an agency-wide dialogue, changes were made in relationships, and some changes were made in the social architecture of CRS" (personal communication, Mar. 30, 2003).

Hills and Dales Child Development Center. This center for physically and mentally disabled children in Dubuque, Iowa, used the Appreciative Inquiry 4-I process as a strategic planning tool to energize its board of directors and engage a larger number of community stakeholders in developing a vision and identifying directions for the future. An internal planning committee led the Appreciative Inquiry process with consultant guidance. Twenty interviewers were trained to inquire by conducting 140 interviews with diverse stakeholders over a six-week period about their best experiences of Hills and Dales and their experiences with its commitment to service. At a Futures Conference that followed, fifty key stakeholders met for a day and a half to imagine and innovate, or design, the future. An internal management team and the board continued to implement the new strategic directions. The Appreciative Inquiry process was deemed successful in achieving consensus on the future (Webb, 1999).

In assessing its impact three years later, the executive director stated,

> One of the ways we found using Appreciative Inquiry has been of tremendous value is in answering the question, "How is what we are doing building a more meaningful life for this person?" I'm so pleased when I hear this approach [is] used as the yardstick by which staff measure their activities, their projects, and their priorities. . . . I can attribute the success of the capital campaign to Appreciative Inquiry. Two years ago, 67 percent of the general public, including business owners and community leaders interviewed, did not know anything about Hills and Dales. These same people, after hearing the story, have given a total of $1.2 million toward our capital campaign. By putting before them the "best of what is possible" visions, we successfully stimulated them to new levels of participation in our community" [J. Imhof, personal communication, Apr. 2003].

Nutrimental Foods. This Brazilian manufacturer of healthy food products, founded in 1968, faced a major crisis after the government, its sole revenue source, decentralized the purchase of food for all federal institutions. The company adapted its products for the consumer market, developed new products, and downsized from 2,000 to 650 employees to stay alive, but was left with a fearful, demoralized workforce. Nutrimental used Appreciative Inquiry to create confidence in its employees and gain a competitive edge in the new markets they were entering. One of the Appreciative Inquiry cofacilitators said, "What the company needed to develop was a breakthrough organization rather than look for breakthrough products . . . something to be built together . . . that no competitor is able to copy" (Marczak, 1998, p. 4).

The company began a whole-system change process in 1997, with guidance from David Cooperrider and a Case Western Reserve University doctoral student, Ilma O. Barros. Barros began the process with a successful pilot Appreciative Inquiry workshop, which led to the launch of an Appreciative Inquiry summit with 750 people—employees and key stakeholders including suppliers, customers, and literate and illiterate workers—where the organization identified best practices and its most important strengths. Cooperrider guided the summit with simultaneous translation, and through the traditional Appreciative Inquiry processes of storytelling, sharing feelings and expectations, and creating the desired future, fully engaged stakeholders. Appreciative Inquiry and the whole-systems change process continues as a way of doing business for Nutrimental Foods.

By 2001, Nutrimental Foods had achieved a 66 percent increase in sales, a 422 percent increase in profitability, and a 42 percent improvement in productivity. It reported that the Appreciative Inquiry process energized the employees and stakeholders and created a "feeling of ownership." A 2000 organization climate survey showed that 91 percent of employees were happy and 95 percent liked their work. The company achieved national status as one of the 100 Best Companies to Work For in Brazil. Organizational leaders attribute their success to "the triple bottom line—people, environment, and profit—all intimately related" (Marczak, 1998).

Evaluation and Appreciative Inquiry

Within the past decade, much has been written about the value of participatory, stakeholder, and learning-oriented approaches to evaluation. Evaluation scholars have recommended that evaluation be more democratic, pluralistic, deliberative, empowering, and enlightening. Evidence of an increasing interest in including stakeholders in evaluation was reported in a study on evaluation use that sought evaluators' feedback using a survey (Preskill and Caracelli, 1997). The authors found that 95 percent of the respondents agreed that "evaluators should take responsibility for involving stakeholders in the evaluation process" (p. 215). When asked to reflect on how important participatory evaluation approaches were ten years ago compared to today, 67 percent said this approach was greatly to extremely more important today. Cousins (2003) provides the following definition of participatory evaluation: "An approach where persons trained in evaluation methods and logic work in collaboration with those not so trained to implement evaluation activities. That is, members of the evaluation community and members of other stakeholder groups relative to the evaluand each participate in some or all of the shaping and/or technical activities required to produce evaluation knowledge leading to judgments of merit and worth and support for program decision making" (p. 245).

By involving stakeholders in the evaluation process, evaluators typically seek to increase the validity of the evaluation data and the use of findings (Brandon, 1998; Cousins and Earl, 1992; Patton, 1997), build evaluation capacity (Compton, Glover-Kudon, Smith, and Avery, 2002; King, 2002; O'Sullivan and O'Sullivan, 1998; Preskill and Torres, 1999), empower individuals and groups to effect social change (Fetterman, 2000; Rebien, 1996), and make evaluation more democratic (Greene, 2000; House and Howe, 1999; MacNeil, 2002; Mathison, 2000). Although the degree of stakeholder participation may vary from one evaluation to another, there is little doubt that evaluators are increasingly involving stakeholders in various phases of evaluation practice (Cousins and

Whitmore, 1998; Ryan and Johnson, 2000; Shulha and Cousins, 1997; Torres and Preskill, 2001; Weiss, 1998).

Evaluators have also been exploring the ways in which stakeholders' learning can be supported and sustained as they participate in evaluation processes (Forss, Rebien, and Carlsson, 2002; Patton, 1997; Preskill and Torres, 1999; Preskill, Zuckerman, and Matthews, forthcoming; Owen and Rogers, 1999; Rossman and Rallis, 2000). By being intentional about learning throughout the evaluation; encouraging dialogue and reflection; questioning assumptions, values, and beliefs; and creating learning spaces and opportunities, individuals may come to more fully understand the evaluand, the organization or community, themselves, each other, and ultimately evaluation practice. The learning that occurs as stakeholders participate in evaluation processes has been called "process use" by Patton (1997), who defines it as "individual changes in thinking and behavior, and program or organizational changes in procedures and culture, that occur among those involved in evaluation as a result of the learning that occurs during the evaluation process. Evidence of process use is represented by the following kind of statement after an evaluation: The impact on our program came not just from the findings but from going through the thinking process that the evaluation required" (p. 90).

Process use reflects social constructivist learning theory in that it focuses on how groups of people make meaning as they conduct an evaluation. The construction, interpretation, and integration of such new knowledge are based on the context of the situation and on participants' experiences (Bruner, 1971; Campbell, 2000; Lave and Wenger, 1991).

Interest in the process of evaluation capacity building has also been growing. The goal here is to help organization and community members understand and develop the knowledge and skills that will enable them to think evaluatively and conduct more internal evaluations. Building evaluation capacity typically entails developing a system and related processes and practices for creating and sustaining evaluation practice within organizations (Stockdill, Baizerman, and Compton, 2002). Evaluation capacity building is often based on participatory approaches to evaluation with an emphasis on learning from the evaluation process and its findings.

Current evaluation practices reflect approaches that are diverse, inclusive of multiple perspectives, and generally supportive of using multiple methods, measures, and criteria. In an effort to refine evaluation practice continually so that evaluation processes and findings are useful and acted on, evaluators continue to explore ways in which evaluation theory and methods can be more effective, while always striving to maintain the integrity of evaluation's logic, process, and findings.

Using Appreciative Inquiry in Evaluation

Appreciative Inquiry is a highly participatory form of inquiry that is often used to address critical organizational issues. As we have considered the underlying assumptions, purposes, and methods of both Appreciative

Inquiry and participatory, stakeholder, and learning-oriented approaches to evaluation, we have come to realize the many similarities. First, both Appreciative Inquiry and collaborative forms of evaluation practice emphasize social constructivism—that sense making and meaning are achieved through dialogue and interaction. Both forms of inquiry stress the significance of asking questions and dialogue. Second, both Appreciative Inquiry and learning-oriented forms of evaluation view inquiry as ongoing, iterative, and integrated into organization and community life. Third, both approaches reflect a systems orientation that includes a structured and planned set of processes. And fourth, both Appreciative Inquiry and participatory, stakeholder, and learning approaches to evaluation stress the use of findings for decision making and action. As proponents of using Appreciative Inquiry in evaluation explain:

> Appreciative Inquiry as a perspective for an evaluation process is grounded in several basic beliefs. The first is the belief that the intervention into any human system is fateful and that the system will move in the direction of the first questions that are asked. In other words, in an evaluation using an appreciative framework, the first questions asked would focus on stories of best practices, positive moments, greatest learnings, successful processes, generative partnerships, and so on. This enables the system to look for its successes and create images of a future built on those positive experiences from the past [Watkins and Mohr, 2001, p. 183].

In surveying the literature, we found several applications of Appreciative Inquiry in conducting evaluations. In some cases, the entire Appreciative Inquiry process was used, while in others the Appreciative Inquiry approach was modified and only partially used. Regardless of the extent to which Appreciative Inquiry was applied, it appears that those who have used it for evaluation purposes have experienced encouraging results.

Elliott (1999) used an appreciative approach to evaluate programs working with street children in Africa. He first included stakeholders in a preparatory workshop where they were introduced to Appreciative Inquiry and developed an appreciative interview protocol. The stakeholders then interviewed the street children, analyzed the resulting data, and developed provocative propositions and actions plans based on their findings. Elliott describes the benefits of using Appreciative Inquiry as the evaluation's overarching philosophy and framework:

> The essence of appreciative inquiry in the context of evaluation is that it gives the organization as a whole a process by which the best practice of the organization can become embedded as the norm against which general practice is tested. In this sense, it is at least as much a teaching and training exercise as it is an evaluative one and therefore has a prolonged beneficial effect on the performance of the organization. This is especially true in an organization which is still unsure of itself, and in which the staff is relatively

inexperienced, for the embedded evaluation to which appreciative inquiry gives access is much less threatening and judgmental than many variants of traditional evaluation for it invites the staff—and indeed, in theory, all the stakeholders—to reflect on their best practice rather than to admit their failures and unsolved problems [pp. 202–203].

Mohr, Smith, and Watkins (2000) conducted an evaluation using Appreciative Inquiry principles within a large pharmaceutical company. They focused on participants gathering information by adapting the generic Appreciative Inquiry protocol and developing provocative propositions. Other adjustments included the consultants conducting many of the interviews themselves and with only some of those within the program being evaluated. Both of these practices differ considerably from full Appreciative Inquiry efforts, where it is desirable for as many program participants to interview each other as possible. The authors and client in this study found that the four generic Appreciative Inquiry questions (peak experiences, personal values, core life-giving factor, and wishes for the future) yielded much richer data than the more traditional evaluation questions and were most valuable in fulfilling the overall goals of the eval-uation. They concluded:

> Appreciative Inquiry does work for evaluation purposes, [for] . . . identifying behavioral changes and . . . as an organizational intervention. The biggest question we had when starting this project was whether Appreciative Inquiry would allow us to answer, to the clients' satisfaction, the fundamental organizational concerns of "how well is this Simulation going and is it a good investment for the corporation?" . . . Not only were these traditional evaluation questions effectively met with this approach, but the corporation benefited from both the learning reinforcement that occurred and the richness of data which would not have been captured in a normal evaluation process [Mohr, Smith, and Watkins, 2000, p. 49].

Odell (2002) has used Appreciative Inquiry in his evaluation work by combining appreciative and participatory approaches in Habitat for Humanity's Measuring Transformation Through Houses program. Within this program, participants developed participatory and appreciatively focused planning, monitoring, and evaluation tools, including qualitative and quantitative reports, surveys, studies, evaluations, and sets of indicators. He explains:

> While the tools of participation and participatory research are relatively well known, the use of Appreciative Inquiry in evaluation and monitoring is relatively new. . . . The Appreciative Inquiry approach is being integrated into Habitat's already "bottom-up" participatory approach to evaluation that is now being used by local Affiliates [in] many other countries beyond Sri Lanka

and Nepal. Together these are already yielding results that are attracting attention in other countries and other organizations [p. 2].

This combined participatory and appreciative approach to planning, monitoring, and evaluation has been successful in tracking the program's achievements and progress in meeting objectives. Odell (2002) reports that the approach also has reduced the negative feelings often associated with evaluation efforts and has increased affiliates' ownership and commitment to monitoring and evaluation processes and to the program overall.

As these three examples illustrate, there are many ways in which Appreciative Inquiry can be applied to evaluation work. To summarize, we provide the following list of situations in which we believe Appreciative Inquiry has the most potential to contribute to evaluation practice:

Contexts
• Where previous evaluation efforts have failed
• Where there is a fear of or skepticism about evaluation
• With varied groups of stakeholders who know little about each other or the program being evaluated
• Within hostile or volatile environments
• When change needs to be accelerated
• When dialogue is critical to moving the organization forward
• When relationships among individuals and groups have deteriorated and there is a sense of hopelessness
• When there is a desire to build evaluation capacity—to help others learn from evaluation practice
• When there is a desire to build a community of practice
• When it is important to increase support for evaluation and possibly the program being evaluated

Process
• To guide an evaluation's design, development, and implementation as an overarching philosophy and framework
• To develop specific data collection methodologies

The use of Appreciative Inquiry in several of these evaluation contexts and processes is explored in Chapters Two through Five.

Reflections on Using Appreciative Inquiry in Evaluation

We believe that using Appreciative Inquiry as an overarching philosophy, approach, or method for evaluation may provide meaningful and useful results. It does this in ways that are similar to participatory approaches to evaluation by stressing the questions asked, viewing inquiry as ongoing and integrated in organizational life, following structured processes, and emphasizing the use of findings. However it is applied, Appreciative Inquiry can also increase participation in the evaluation, maximize the use of results, and build capacity for learning and change within organizations and communities. By focusing on exceptional performance, it creates continuous opportunities to look back on those moments of excellence and use them to guide the organization toward a more positive future.

Although Appreciative Inquiry has been used in several evaluation studies, the literature so far has not addressed some of the more complex issues, such as the appropriate circumstances for using Appreciative Inquiry in evaluation, the advantages and disadvantages of doing so, and the lessons learned from these evaluations. Many of these and other issues are addressed in the following chapters.

References

Ashford, G., and Patkar, S. *The Positive Path: Using Appreciative Inquiry in Rural Indian Communities.* Winnipeg, Manitoba: International Institute for Sustainable Development, 2001.

Banaga, G. "A Spiritual Path to Organizational Renewal." In S. A. Hammond and C. Royal (eds.), *Lessons from the Field: Applying Appreciative Inquiry.* Plano, Tex.: Practical Press, 1998.

Brandon, P. R. "Stakeholder Participation for the Purpose of Helping Ensure Evaluation Validity: Bridging the Gap Between Collaborative and Non-Collaborative Evaluations." *American Journal of Evaluation,* 1998, *19*(3), 325–337.

Bruner, J. *Toward a Theory of Instruction.* Cambridge, Mass.: Harvard University Press, 1971.

Campbell, D. *The Socially Constructed Organization.* London: H. Karnac Books, 2000.

Compton, D. W., Glover-Kudon, R., Smith, I. E., and Avery, M. E. "Ongoing Capacity Building in the American Cancer Society." In D. W. Compton, M. Baizerman, and S. H. Stockdill (eds.), *The Art, Craft, and Science of Evaluation Capacity Building.* New Directions for Evaluation, no. 93. San Francisco: Jossey-Bass, 2002.

Cooperrider, D. L., and Whitney, D. "A Positive Revolution in Change: Appreciative Inquiry." In D. Cooperrider, P. F. Sorensen, D. Whitney, and T. F. Yaeger (eds.), *Appreciative Inquiry: Rethinking Human Organization Toward a Positive Theory of Change.* Champaign, Ill.: Stipes Publishing, 2000.

Cooperrider, D. L., Whitney, D., and Stavros, J. M. *Appreciative Inquiry Handbook.* Bedford Heights, Ohio: Lakeshore Publishers, 2003.

Cousins, J. B. "Utilization Effects of Participatory Evaluation." In T. Kellaghan and D. L. Stufflebeam (eds.), *International Handbook of Educational Evaluation.* Norwell, Mass.: Kluwer, 2003.

Cousins, J. B., and Earl, L. M. "The Case for Participatory Evaluation." *Educational Evaluation and Policy Analysis,* 1992, *14*(4), 397–418.

Cousins, J. B., and Whitmore, E. "Framing Participatory Evaluation." In E. Whitmore (ed.), *Understanding and Practicing Participatory Evaluation.* New Directions for Evaluation, no. 80. San Francisco: Jossey-Bass, 1998.

Elliott, C. *Locating the Energy for Change: An Introduction to Appreciative Inquiry.* Winnipeg, Manitoba: International Institute for Sustainable Development, 1999.

Fetterman, D. M. *Foundations of Empowerment Evaluation: Step by Step.* Thousand Oaks, Calif.: Sage, 2000.

Forss, K., Rebien, C. C., and Carlsson, J. "Process Use of Evaluations." *Evaluation,* 2002, *8*(1), 29–45.

Gergen, K. J. *Toward Transformation in Social Knowledge.* Thousand Oaks, Calif.: Sage, 1994. (Originally published 1982.)

Greene, J. C. "Challenges in Practicing Deliberative Democratic Evaluation." In K. E. Ryan and L. DeStefano (eds.), *Evaluation as a Democratic Process: Promoting Inclusion, Dialogue, and Deliberation.* New Directions for Evaluation, no. 85. San Francisco: Jossey-Bass, 2000.

Hammond, S. A. *Thin Book on Appreciative Inquiry.* Plano, Tex.: Thin Book Publishing, 1996.

House, E., and Howe, K. R. *Values in Evaluation and Social Research.* Thousand Oaks, Calif.: Sage, 1999.

King, J. "Building the Evaluation Capacity of a School District." In D. W. Compton, M. Baizerman, and S. H. Stockdill (eds.), *The Art, Craft, and Science of Evaluation Capacity Building.* New Directions for Evaluation, no. 93. San Francisco: Jossey-Bass, 2002.

Lave, J., and Wenger, E. *Situated Learning: Legitimate Peripheral Participation.* Cambridge: Cambridge University Press, 1991.

MacNeil, C. "Evaluator as Steward of Citizen Deliberation." *American Journal of Evaluation,* 2002, 23(1), 45–54.

Marczak, L. "Appreciative Inquiry at Nutrimental—How Did It Happen?" Sept. 1998. [http://connection.cwru.edu/ai/practice/organizationDetail.cfm?coid=172&sector=27.]

Mathison, S. "Deliberation, Evaluation, and Democracy." In K. E. Ryan and L. DeStefano (eds.), *Evaluation as a Democratic Process: Promoting Inclusion, Dialogue, and Deliberation.* New Directions for Evaluation, no. 85. San Francisco: Jossey-Bass, 2000.

Mohr, B. J., Smith, E., and Watkins, J. M. "Appreciative Inquiry and Learning Assessment: An Embedded Evaluation Process in a Transitional Pharmaceutical Company." *OD Practitioner,* 2000, 32(1), 36–52.

Odell, M. *"Beyond the Box": An Innovative Habitat for Humanity Paradigm for Participatory Planning, Monitoring and Evaluation—Measuring and Increasing Program Impacts with Appreciative Inquiry.* Americus, Ga.: Habitat for Humanity International, 2002.

O'Sullivan, R. G., and O'Sullivan, J. M. "Evaluation Voices: Promoting Evaluation from Within Programs Through Collaboration." *Evaluation and Program Planning,* 1998, 21, 21–29.

Owen, J. M., and Rogers, P. *Program Evaluation: Forms and Approaches.* Thousand Oaks, Calif.: Sage, 1999.

Patton, M. Q. *Utilization-Focused Evaluation: The New Century Text.* (3rd ed.) Thousand Oaks, Calif.: Sage, 1997.

Preskill, H., and Caracelli, V. "Current and Developing Conceptions of Use: Evaluation Use TIG Survey Results." *Evaluation Practice,* 1997, 18(3), 209–225.

Preskill, H., and Torres, R. T. *Evaluative Inquiry for Learning in Organizations.* Thousand Oaks, Calif.: Sage, 1999.

Preskill, H., Zuckerman, B., and Matthews, B. *An Exploratory Study of Process Use: Findings and Implications for Future Research.* American Journal of Evaluation, forthcoming, 24(4).

Rebien, C. C. "Participatory Evaluation of Development Assistance." *Evaluation,* 1996, 2(2), 151–171.

Rossman, G. B., and Rallis, S. F. "Critical Inquiry and Use as Action." In V. J. Caracelli and H. Preskill (eds.), *The Expanding Scope of Evaluation Use.* New Directions for Evaluation, no. 88. San Francisco: Jossey-Bass, 2000.

Ryan, K. E., and Johnson, T. D. "Democratizing Evaluation: Meanings and Methods from Practice." In K. E. Ryan and L. DeStefano (eds.), *Evaluation as a Democratic Process: Promoting Inclusion, Dialogue, and Deliberation.* New Directions for Evaluation, no. 85. San Francisco: Jossey-Bass, 2000.

Shulha, L., and Cousins, B. "Evaluation Use: Theory, Research, and Practice Since 1986." *Evaluation Practice,* 1997, 18(3), 195–208.

Stockdill, S. H., Baizerman, M., and Compton, D. W. "Toward a Definition of the ECB Process: A Conversation with the Literature." In D. W. Compton, M. Baizerman, and S. H. Stockdill (eds.), *The Art, Craft, and Science of Evaluation Capacity Building.* New Directions for Evaluation, no. 93. San Francisco: Jossey-Bass, 2002.

Torres, R. T., and Preskill, H. "Evaluation and Organizational Learning: Past, Present, and Future." *American Journal of Evaluation,* 2001, 22(3), 387–396.

Watkins, J., and Mohr, B. *Appreciative Inquiry: Change at the Speed of Imagination.* San Francisco: Jossey-Bass/Pfeiffer, 2001.

Webb, L. "Appreciative Inquiry as a Way to Jump Start Change." *At Work,* 1999, 8(2), 1–3.

Weiss, C. H. *Evaluation.* (2nd ed.) Upper Saddle River, N.J.: Prentice Hall, 1998.

Whitney, D., and Trosten-Bloom, A. *The Power of Appreciative Inquiry.* San Francisco: Berrett-Koehler, 2003.

ANNE T. COGHLAN is an independent evaluation consultant based in Dhaka, Bangladesh.

HALLIE PRESKILL is professor of organizational learning and instructional technologies at the University of New Mexico.

TESSIE TZAVARAS CATSAMBAS is president of EnCompass LLC in Bethesda, Maryland.

2

The case in this chapter illustrates how using the language of strengths, values, and ideals can help participants take stock of their program in order to move forward what they most value in the process of curricular reform and collaborative working relations.

Appreciative Evaluation Within a Conflicted Educational Context

Sheila McNamee

This chapter describes the use of Appreciative Inquiry in the evaluation of an academic department at a private high school. The evaluation process was commissioned by the dean of faculty and the department chair to assess two related issues: the department's curriculum and its abilities to work collaboratively. The goal of evaluation, part of a schoolwide curriculum reform process, was to assess the department's curriculum in such a manner that its strengths could be noted and built on while its weaknesses could be eliminated or at least diminished. To that end, those who might benefit from the evaluation were the department faculty, the students, and ultimately the school.

Evaluation as Social Construction

My view of evaluation, which places emphasis on evaluation as an ongoing process, emerges from my social constructionist orientation (Gergen, 1999; McNamee and Gergen, 1999). Briefly, constructionism focuses our attention on the social processes by which people create and maintain realities. This entails focusing on what people do together. Consequently, constructionists focus attention on language practices (all embodied activities of persons relating together). Constructionism proposes that the most important aspect of social life is what people do together because in their joint actions, they create a world that values certain beliefs and practices. Since we all inhabit many different relationships and communities (not to mention the access we have to worlds we do not literally inhabit through globalization and technological advancement), the potential for constructing very diverse and incompatible ways of being in the world is great. Thus, we should not be surprised when people come together in a context like the one examined in this chapter with

NEW DIRECTIONS FOR EVALUATION, no. 100, Winter 2003 © Wiley Periodicals, Inc.

conflicting values, beliefs, and realities. The challenge is one of coordinating multiple ways of being, and one way to do this is to invite participants into a dialogue where they learn to become curious about each other's differences. This curiosity generates a sense of respect for ways of being that are incompatible with one's own. Participants can respect the coherence of another's position while simultaneously disagreeing with it. This respect in turn fosters an ability to remain in conversation, which is essential in a social constructivist context.

Appreciative Inquiry as One Elaboration of Social Construction in Practice

I see Appreciative Inquiry as a useful elaboration of social construction. If what we do together creates the possibilities and constraints within which we live, then how might our realities change if we replace deficit-based language, which focuses on what is not working, with talk of what is working? I am interested in exploring how approaching evaluation from an appreciative stance might invite participants to engage in program improvement and development. I am also interested in exploring how such an approach to evaluation might assist participants in reconstructing their working relationships so that their differences are respected and they value themselves and each other for the specific talents each one offers to their collective program.

The question we need to explore is what we might gain by focusing our evaluation on those aspects of programs that we appreciate: those parts that are working and are valued and that invite program participants into coordinating a generative future together. I am not interested in claiming that appreciatively oriented evaluation is inherently better than more standard forms of evaluation. Rather, I see appreciative evaluation, which is conducted within the discourse of appreciation and strengths, as a version of formative evaluation; it is evaluation that is conducted with the purpose of improving the program. Furthermore, the evaluation process itself becomes part of the improvement of the program. My interest is in exploring appreciative evaluation as a potentially generative assessment tool by virtue of the propensity of appreciatively oriented conversation to yield creative possibilities for coordination. Thus, it seems possible that programs evaluated within an appreciative frame might ultimately become more humane and, by association, more socially useful. The case presented here is one excursion into this issue and by no means is presented as definitive proof that appreciative evaluation is better, more successful, or more useful than traditional forms of evaluation. My aim is only to raise questions and open possibilities.

Introduction to the Case

Taking an appreciative approach to the evaluation of one academic department in a private high school enabled an emphasis on the resources and strengths of the department and its curriculum. It was assumed that this stance might be different enough from previously used evaluation processes to encourage and enable the needed transformation and improvement of both curriculum and departmental working style.

Curricular problems noted during previous reviews included a lack of coherence in assignments from one grade to the next, pedagogical inconsistency from teacher to teacher, outdated reading lists, and ongoing debates among the faculty concerning programmatic philosophy. These difficulties were accentuated by a working environment in which collegial, professional trust and respect were always in question. According to department faculty, "camps" were formed and strategies concocted for making pedagogical and personnel decisions. Each prior evaluation had left the department feeling inadequate, overworked, and more entrenched in its divisiveness. Self-reports provided by each faculty member, the department chair, and the dean of faculty acknowledged that previous evaluations had not led to any generative programmatic improvement. For this reason, evaluation conducted within an appreciative stance was viewed as potentially useful for the school, the department, the faculty, and ultimately the students.

Although the department chair, the dean, and a small number of departmental faculty were eager to embark on an evaluative process that was generated within an appreciative context, most of the faculty were reluctant to spend time on any activity that purported to improve the professional and interpersonal functioning of the department. Like most other long-term working groups, the faculty were deeply settled into their oppositional positions and greatly resisted spending time on this effort (time that would be taken from their families, friends, athletic and club obligations to the school, and course preparation time).

Appreciative Evaluation

To direct the evaluation toward Appreciative Inquiry into the department's curriculum and working style, I designed a procedure that used one-on-one interviews followed by a two-day retreat. After initial contact with the chair of the department to discuss the use of an appreciative approach, I was introduced to the entire faculty at the first meeting of the academic year. During this introduction, I explained that my intention was not to evaluate their program and working style from my perspective but rather to invite them into a conversation with me about how best to evaluate their program and their working style as a group. I described my interest in working from discussions of what they value in their program and in their collegial relationships as opposed to engaging in detailed explorations of what was not working or what they did not like. I explained that I understood there already was a good deal of both open and private discussion about problems and their causes. In addition, I noted that although those sorts of conversations can be useful and often help to clarify and thereby improve a program, that had not been the case for this department (by their own admission). Therefore, my attempt would be to bracket discussions of problems and causality and place the spotlight on how to build on the curricular and collegial strengths that already were acknowledged within the program.

I explained that my intention was not to find a way to "make them all get along with each other." Rather, my hope was that a by-product of our collaborative evaluation would be a respect for differences that would promote new ways of coordinating their work activities together in a more generative and harmonious manner. In addition, the department would begin to develop more collaborative, respectful working relations by virtue of their participation in the joint creation of the evaluation. I invited each member of the department to contact me with any questions, concerns, or suggestions.

I immediately began scheduling thirty-minute meetings with each faculty member. Prior to these one-on-one meetings, I sent each person a list of questions on which to reflect in preparation for our discussion (see Exhibit 2.1). These questions were designed to generate reflection prior to the interviews. During the interviews, I did not methodically go through the list of questions with each faculty member. Instead, I began each interview by asking faculty to tell me what he or she thought I most needed to know about the department, the curriculum, and the working relationships of members. I asked each member to describe the department at its best and to comment on the values, strengths, and talents each person brings to the department. I also asked what values, strengths, and talents faculty imagined their colleagues would associate with their own unique contribution to the program.

As might be expected, my interviews did not omit discussion of departmental or personal problems. Many faculty seemed to view their interviews with me as a chance to air their side of the story. This raises an interesting issue for me as a constructionist using Appreciative Inquiry as a method for constructing transformation. Many mistakenly believe that Appreciative Inquiry prohibits any discussion or talk of problems. In my own experience, prohibiting the very issues that people want to discuss is oppressive and therefore monologic. Sampson (1993) describes monologism as a particular way of engaging with others where one sees the other as separate and in the service of oneself. Dialogism, in contrast, celebrates the coordination of all participants in the conversation and recognizes the mutual dependence participants have on each other to construct the worlds in which they live. One does not need to be monologic and eliminate all problem talk from the conversation in order to engage in Appreciative Inquiry. I find that when people feel they have had a chance to tell their story and it has been heard, they are very willing to experiment with talking in a different way. In this case, the different talk is appreciative.

When faculty wanted to talk about problems with me, I did not try to redirect the conversation. I was fascinated, given the history of this group, by their difficult interpersonal relationships and the fact that although I had been hired by the chair of the department (who was not outside the

Exhibit 2.1. Preparation Questions for the Interviews and Discussions

I appreciate your taking the time to meet with me before the retreat so that we can get to know each other. Additionally, it is important to me that I have the chance to understand how you see the current curricular issues you confront, the situation within your department, as well as within the school in general. Please feel free to share with me anything that you think might be useful in reaching the goal of the retreat.

Before we meet, I thought it might be useful for you to think about some of the general issues about which I will be asking. Feel free to think about answers to the following questions. Use these questions in whatever way you find useful.

1. How would you characterize yourself as a member of this department? Can you describe your relationship to the department and to the school? If you can think of a story that conveys who you are in these relationships, that would be useful to me in understanding you and your relationships with the group.
2. Have you heard or experienced conversations within the school—at any level— related to how your department operates and envisions itself that have been especially constructive? What do you think made these conversations constructive? Additionally, what does the usual conversation within the department (about how to be a department) focus on? What topics, questions, or information are usually avoided or excluded, which are useful, and so forth?
3. As you think about the retreat, what could happen there that would lead you to feel that your participation was worthwhile, and what could happen afterward that would make you happy to have been part of the group discussion? What do you most care that I keep in mind during the retreat? From your perspective, what topics are most important for discussion during the retreat to make it successful?
4. What might be set in place to enable you to speak as fully as you wish at the retreat? Can you suggest any guidelines for communicating that represent your own commitments to speak and listen in ways that support the general purpose of the retreat?
5. What do you want your colleagues to understand about who you are and what you most care about around the issue of department identity and practice? What questions do you hope that others might ask you? What do you really want to understand about your departmental colleagues and their concerns? What might you ask others in order to get some clarity about these things?
6. Do you have any further questions or comments for me?

fray of hostile histories) they willingly offered detailed accounts of the relational politics within the department. In fact, in one interview I commented on how appreciative I was that everyone was being so honest and trusting me with some very sensitive information. The person I was interviewing at the time responded, "But you told us we should trust you!" As the outside evaluator, this was a confirming moment, and I wonder how much I can credit the trustworthiness I embodied with this group to the time-consuming task of meeting individually with each member of the faculty. By beginning each interview with my vow of confidentiality and by giving my time to get to know each one personally, I was able to listen to the problems, acknowledge that they had been heard, and move each person on to a discussion of strengths, values, and high points.

It is these strengths, values, and high points that remained the focus of my work with the department. I began by pulling out the overlapping themes that emerged from my individual interviews in preparation for the retreat:

- The department's focus on history and tradition versus change
- Evaluation of each other as faculty and of students
- Commitment to a common but broad pedagogical frame versus the teacher's autonomy and independence in the classroom
- The decision-making process and the need for and meaning of agreement and consensus
- What it means to be a good colleague
- The unifying power of discussing intellectual passions
- The need for ritualistic celebration of each other's achievements

These themes reemerged during the retreat working sessions and will be discussed later in this chapter.

Immediately before the retreat, faculty were asked to reflect on additional issues in order to prepare them for work on evaluating their current curriculum and working style. These issues, beyond preparing them to engage in the evaluation that would transpire at the retreat, were designed to orient the group toward a collaborative mode of work. In an expansion of the typical application of Appreciative Inquiry, faculty were asked to think about and be ready to share their personal statement of teaching. To assist them in this task, they were given the following questions:

- How did you come into the profession of teaching? What captured your imagination about this life choice?
- What drew you to the idea of working with students?
- What ideas did you have about working with colleagues?
- What attracted you to this particular school?
- How would you describe your overall teaching objectives and goals?
- Provide an anecdote or story that will capture for the group your teaching methods.

These questions were designed to spark stories of high points (as in typical Appreciative Inquiry). However, the high points were not about the department or school as a whole but about each faculty member's own passion for teaching. Consistent with Appreciative Inquiry, the assumption was made that sharing stories of one's own love of and excitement about teaching could serve as an initiation into a different and transformative conversation among colleagues. This is contrasted to a more standard inquiry into teaching philosophy that would generally yield a set of abstract principles. The stories each member told gave life and coherence to what would otherwise be disembodied knowledge.

The Retreat

Prior to selecting someone to conduct the evaluation for this group, the chair had announced to the faculty that they would be required to participate in a three-day retreat in the fall designed to evaluate their program and working style. The retreat was held at a resort on the beach with many recreational facilities such as golfing, tennis, and beautiful walking paths. The retreat began on Sunday afternoon and ended with lunch on Tuesday.

Most faculty were quite clear in their interviews with me that either they felt the retreat would be a waste of their time or that they were willing to attend but would be exceedingly upset if the end product was not a new curriculum or some concrete movement toward one. The general sentiment was that being sequestered away from family, teaching obligations, and extracurricular responsibilities was going beyond normal expectations for the job. (Each faculty member, by school design, coaches or directs some extracurricular activity, and this retreat interfered with several athletic play-off games.) The majority of the faculty resented the idea of the retreat. Many were willing to go but were also ready to resent being forced into this activity if it turned out to be another situation where a lot of good conversation transpired with no subsequent action. The department chair had cancelled all Monday classes and those for Tuesday morning. This could have been an additional difficulty for faculty who felt they were losing precious classroom time. The majority did not share the chair's idea that this would be a relaxing benefit for the faculty.

The design of the retreat was generated in collaboration with the department's Self Study Subcommittee, appointed as part of the schoolwide curriculum assessment procedure. Each department had its own working subcommittee focused on the details of its own department. These subcommittees would meet together periodically to discuss the broader issues of the schoolwide curriculum. The department's subcommittee had been meeting for several months and had gathered numerous documents to review in assessing and redesigning curriculum. As the evaluator hired to conduct the overall evaluation of both the department's curriculum and working style, I assumed that my job required coordination with the Self Study Subcommittee since they were already engaged in the process of evaluating the departmental curriculum. Several weeks prior to the retreat, we collaborated in designing that time together in such a way that the materials and issues generated by the Self Study Subcommittee were integrated with the issues generated in my interviews with faculty. The design focused on central questions.

Setting the Context. During the opening portion of the retreat, faculty were asked to share the story of how they entered into the profession of teaching. The storytelling, which took over two hours, created an atmosphere of respect and interest and generated a good deal of humor. After a dinner break, the conversation continued.

"Who Are We, and Who Can We Become?" Drawing on the personal stories of teaching, I invited the faculty to select someone else in the group (preferably someone with whom they typically had little interaction) and interview each other about high points in teaching ("Tell me a story about a high point for you as a teacher") as well as about the values and strengths about themselves as teachers that their stories reflected ("As you tell that story, what are you reminded of as your own values and strengths?"). In relation to the 4-D model described in Chapter One, this activity would be considered the Discovery phase of Appreciative Inquiry (appreciating that which gives life).

Each pair found a comfortable spot in the large room within which we were working to conduct the interviews. When the interviews were completed (after about forty-five minutes), the group reconvened, and each pair reported the values and strengths identified through the stories told. I created a list on newsprint as each pair shared the values and strengths that had emerged in their conversation. This list was incorporated in the final report. In this manner, the faculty had a written record of their collective and personal strengths and values.

The faculty described many strengths, values, and talents among themselves, which are set out in Exhibit 2.2, in relation to themselves as professionals, to students, and to each other as colleagues. They reported valuing each other mostly for the commitment and passion each brings to teaching. They agreed that the integrity and quality of the student-teacher relationship is of central concern to them all. In general, the faculty described themselves at their best when talking about their academic work. In addition, there was agreement that they are most energized when exchanging ideas and innovations for teaching, classroom exercises, assignments, and projects. The image that emerged was one of a group of people who love what they do for a living and enjoy the chance to share their ideas with each other.

"Describe the Features That Would Help You Create an Ideal Curriculum." A brainstorming session followed the discussion of values, strengths, and talents. The idea here was to build on the identified attributes in fantasizing specific features that would help create the ideal curriculum and working relationships. Here, we moved into the Dream phase of Appreciative Inquiry (envisioning what might be). Participants were invited to call out the features that would help them create an ideal curriculum. Their ideas were listed on newsprint and integrated into the final report for their future use.

Several areas were identified (for a full list, see Exhibit 2.3): curricular, structural aspects of the program, physical resources, human resources, and school policy. The general tenor of the conversation articulated the need for

Exhibit 2.2.   Strengths, Values, and Talents of the Department Faculty

As Faculty and Professionals
- Passionate learners
- Appreciate power of personal stories
- Teach students to observe their place in the world
- Willingness to travel where students take us
- Communicative enthusiasm (without taking over)
- Teach integrity to each other and to our students
- Thoughtful editing
- Not fixated on specific genres
- Not content oriented
- Open and flexible
- Value students as multidimensional (holistic appreciation of students)
- Privilege the process of engaging with a text
- Dedicated to doing best for students
- Fine sense of humor
- Willingness to give to students
- Diversity of experiences (as department faculty)
- Willing to take emotional and intellectual chances
- Creativity in teaching
- Like adolescents
- Not indulgent to the students
- Respectfulness for new ideas/vocation (from a sense of deep seated self-confidence)

In Relation to Students
- Try to hear—pay attention to what students are saying
- Get kids to go beyond their expectations
- Appreciate power of personal stories
- Teach students to observe their place in the world
- Willingness to travel where students take us
- Communicative enthusiasm (without taking over)
- Teach integrity to our students
- Thoughtful editing
- Close readers for students
- Open and flexible
- Value students as multidimensional (holistic appreciation of students)
- Empower students through our teaching method
- Privilege process of engaging with a text
- Let students explore diversity (through personal narrative)
- Dedicated to doing best for students

In Relation to Each Other as Colleagues
- Control academic egos
- Listen
- Generous with each other regarding teaching—share well
- Appreciate power of personal stories
- Talking about texts (as colleagues, we listen to each other)
- Colleagues who practice what we ask our students to practice
- Teach integrity to each other
- Close readers for each other
- Open and flexible
- Ability to jar each other out of complacency
- Best when not insular—comfortable place to be—open door

Exhibit 2.3. Central Features of an Ideal Program

Curricular Issues
- Students write all the time
- Faculty give immediate feedback all the time
- Experiential education beyond the classroom
- Classroom-life connection with service-learning
- Student radio show (service-learning)—"Reporter at Large" as a genre
- Immersion experience in one topic or discipline

Structural Aspects
- Opportunity to meet with students as many hours as needed
- No e-mail or voice mail used to conduct our work
- E-mail used for the majority of our business
- Find a way to realize the ideal.

Resources (Space and Equipment)
- Everyone has a classroom
- Common room with fireplace that would hold everyone
- Everyone has own computer
- Departmental library
- State-of-the-art DVD and theater
- Department facility for editing DVD

Human Resources
- Departmental secretary

School Policies
- No tenure
- Ongoing evaluation and accountability
- Fat blocks (longer teaching formats)
- Three classes a week
- Narrative feedback to replace letter grades
- Free weekends
- Interdisciplinary opportunities
- The school would create and honor time for reflection
- A stronger commitment to faculty enrichment

departmental teaching to have ample time, commitment, and one-on-one contact between student and teacher. A central feature of the ideal curriculum would be constant and active revision of students' work urged on by teacher and peer commentary and feedback. The faculty ideally envisioned a program that reached beyond the mechanics of the discipline and engaged students by integrating their own experiences.

The Curriculum. At the start of the next day, we moved from the Dream phase to the Design phase of our inquiry. Faculty worked in five separate groups (quasi-randomly assigned) to coconstruct their future. There were five faculty who were new to the department at the time of the retreat. Because they had not yet been acculturated into the political and philosophical divisions in the department, I invited them to each serve as a representative of a different group. I asked each of the five to randomly draw names from a hat to determine their group membership. It was interesting to me to note how much all the faculty liked this technique for forming working groups. I connected it with a ritual I had been told about in the department: the youngest member of the faculty would light the fire at the first faculty party in the fall. However, given a number of unfortunate circumstances, there had not been a full faculty party for several years. In introducing the five newest and youngest members of the faculty to draw names for the group composition, I described the process as my attempt to maintain the ritual within the department. I think the randomness of the group formation relieved many warring faculty. Yet I also think that integrating the new with the old (new members leading older members, as well as a new procedure following an old ritual) opened a space where faculty could all be genuinely together.

Each group was instructed to find a comfortable space and brainstorm an answer to the following question: What is the ideal program for this school? Round tables for working, flip charts, and markers were provided. In order to get the conversation going, groups were given the following instructions:

- Suspend any existing notions of structure. Do not assume that the class schedule or current sequencing of courses is in place since anything could change by virtue of the curriculum revisions currently under discussion.
- Really try to think beyond what exists, what has been done in the past, or what you think someone might think you should be doing.
- Think about what is really important to teach students.
- Think about what is essential.
- Think about what could fit any specific curricular design.

The discussion took approximately one hour.

The five plans were presented after lunch. Each group provided an overview of the plan it had designed for the ideal curriculum. Debate and discussion of plans were not allowed, but everyone was encouraged to ask questions to gain further information and clarification. After all five ideal programs were presented, five newly formed groups worked on developing an integration of these five. Each group had a representative from each of the five original groups. Thus, each of the new groups had one member who could speak directly to each plan. Groups were instructed to select, merge, integrate, and synthesize the five working plans into one plan. Materials and documents about the current program (documents written for previous reviews and for school publicity) as well as documents generated by the Self Study Committee were available for use.

This discussion yielded five proposed integrated ideal plans. Each was presented in the same format as the first plans were presented. This was followed by a whole group discussion of the ideal plans, which resulted in one integrated design (largely due to the fact that each integrated plan was quite similar). Through this process, the faculty realized that their images of their program were not as disparate as they had believed.

Integration of Ideal Curriculum: Creating a Plan of Action. The ideal program embraced several core commitments that were reflective of the values and strengths faculty had identified in the first session of the retreat. Their commitments were to teaching and high expectations for students' work. Central to these commitments was opportunity for close student-teacher engagement, teaching a diverse range of subtopics, and daily writing that would serve several purposes (for example, self-knowledge, discovery, understanding of deadlines). The curriculum in the ideal program embodied several necessary elements relevant to classroom management, student skill acquisition, and assignments. (For the final document, see the chapter appendix.)

The structure of the ideal curriculum focused on issues of classroom management; resources that would enhance teaching, the school, and the department structure; and assignments and grading. Some of the highlights included a reduced teaching load, thereby allowing for more student conference time, creation of a computer and working lab, and narrative assessment (as opposed to letter or numerical grades).

In addition, faculty were interested in exploring (and having the time to explore) the importance of teaching various topics and employing a range of pedagogical methods. Specifically, the emphasis was placed on the need for an extended conversation on what counts as useful pedagogies. Members of the department defined teaching methods differently. It was only in the context of appreciative, interested inquiry that members of the department learned that what they previously thought were distinct philosophical and practical distinctions were actually issues around which they were in complete agreement with each other. It was agreed that a discussion about these perceived differences would be necessary as the faculty worked toward evaluating and improving their curriculum.

Relatedly, the issue of teacher autonomy and what it means to value autonomy was raised. This issue seemed to touch on the heart of the communication issues in the department. Significant topics were brought to the table, such as what is lost and what is gained in celebrating autonomy, how teachers' autonomy is beneficial (or not) for students, how autonomy figures in pretenure evaluations, and the relationship between autonomy and trust. In the ideal curriculum, the issue of autonomy would be openly discussed and clarified.

Faculty agreed that in their ideal curriculum, there would be ample time for teaching and working with students. They would have a common vocabulary worked out so that they could provide students with consistency as they move through the curriculum. And finally, faculty agreed that the ideal program would have clarity concerning the connection between the various aspects of the discipline.

Committing to the Next Steps. On the final morning, the synthesis of the discussion concerning the plan of action was distributed to the faculty. In general, this synthesis represented a sense of commitment and agreement by the faculty, thereby serving as an organizing and orienting guide for refining the current curriculum. The recurrent themes that had emerged in my individual interviews with each faculty member were presented to the group at this time. This presentation and open discussion was intended to offer the opportunity for the group to publicly acknowledge issues that were relevant to the evaluation of both the curriculum and their working relations. It was important for the faculty to consider the recurrent themes as they developed concrete ways in which to use the information emerging from our collaborative evaluation in the development of their curriculum and more effective working relationships. The emergent themes were acknowledged by the group as ongoing issues within the department and therefore connected to the current challenges of redesigning the curriculum and the group's work style. This open discussion led to a concluding session where the faculty committed themselves to a specific set of actions.

Actions Agreed on at the Close of the Retreat. The final phase of the retreat embraced the Delivery phase of Appreciative Inquiry. Here, faculty engaged in a conversation about how to realize the program they imagined. The faculty agreed to four immediate steps as a result of having engaged in the appreciative evaluation:

1. Creating a committee to explore the faculty evaluation and tenure process and draft proposed alterations to the process
2. Initiating ongoing classroom observations where the resulting suggestions for individual faculty members' teaching and for the departmental curriculum would be actively discussed
3. Creating an agenda committee to prioritize actions, ideas, and discussions that emerged from the retreat
4. Committing to direct communication with each other concerning professional or personal concerns

Reflections on the Process of Appreciative Evaluation

We can see from the action steps agreed on at the end of the evaluation process that the faculty had come to a collective understanding of their curriculum and a vision of where they should be heading. This is not to suggest that there was absolute agreement about the curriculum or about how they work together as a group. However, the themes that emerged in my interviews echoed throughout the retreat discussions (throughout the evaluation) and seemed to open the possibility for new conversations and new ways of constructing a strong curriculum.

As for evaluating the working relationships among the faculty, the evaluation process engaged them in not only new conversations about what they value, what works, and what they see as strengths in each other and their curriculum but also in new ways to be in conversation with each other. The stories told at the start of the retreat provided a dramatically different context within which colleagues could discuss what had previously been a difficult topic. Each person was invited into each other's passion and joy for teaching. Each was given the opportunity to recognize similarities between self and other. And each was afforded the chance to see the other in a frame that differed dramatically from the distrusting and disrespectful frame of everyday departmental activities.

The results of this very different conversation and very different approach to program evaluation were identified in follow-up conversations with the faculty. They reported that their perceived differences were actually smaller than they had imagined. They also reported that the process of examining their curriculum in the manner we did allowed them the opportunity to engage with each other in ways that were new and useful. Rather than making negative judgmental assessments of their curriculum or their working style (or of each other!), they engaged in conversations that were effectively different. They were taking stock of (evaluating) what worked, what they valued, and what their strengths were.

After providing a report to the dean of faculty, the department chair, and each faculty member, I met with the dean and chair to discuss their responses to the summary of the retreat. This discussion began a dialogue concerning the ways in which the school's administration could assist the department in making the desired changes. Follow-up conversations with the department chair and the faculty indicate that they have developed new procedures for faculty evaluation and are in the process of trying out these procedures. They report that the annual faculty evaluation has taken on an exciting new tenor because of the conversations they have had, the procedures with which they are experimenting, and the feeling that this process is ongoing and flexible.

As part of the process of peer evaluation and also of curriculum development, the faculty have initiated classroom observation and feedback sessions. In discussing feedback from faculty, they report a more collegial sense of the annual review process. My sense is that the simple act of openly discussing the review procedures has changed the way in which both senior and junior faculty approach evaluative reviews. They report ongoing conversations to alter the actual method of review, but to this point, the methods appear the same but the experience is different. These discussions also yielded energetic discussions concerning pedagogical issues such as course content, course sequencing, and teaching styles, thereby assisting in the further development of the "ideal" curriculum. The department reports that they have a well-functioning agenda committee that reviews all issues within the department's operation and prioritizes discussions and actions among the faculty. The combination of these three actions (all agreed on at the close of the evaluation retreat) has assisted the department in realizing (thus far) their fourth action goal: direct communication with each other concerning professional and personal concerns. It seems that the different conversations—conversations that were initiated with personal stories and developed into dialogue about strengths, values, and ideals—helped to create different ways of interacting among the faculty. Whereas they assessed their working relationships and style of working in negative terms prior to this evaluation, they now have a more inspired assessment of who they are as a group and how they work together. In effect, they report respecting disagreements on issues and becoming curious rather than judgmental about them.

Concluding Thoughts

Appreciative evaluation commonly is critiqued because it is believed to ignore problems within a program. Yet the fact is that problems and weaknesses are often much easier to address when evaluation takes an appreciative stance. Since appreciatively oriented evaluation begins by taking stock of resources, values, and strengths, those participating in the evaluation feel better equipped to address difficulties and problems. Often what have appeared to be immutable problems (such as the lack of trust and respect among the faculty in this case study) are viewed within a context of possibility rather than failure. Evaluation that emanates from an appreciative stance does not have to ignore aspects of programs that are not working well. The point is not to avoid such topics but rather to mine the resources and strengths that are part of the program in order to improve or in some way alter the parts that are not working.

In addition, and as this case suggests, evaluation from an appreciative stance can facilitate collaboration among participants. Appreciatively oriented evaluation provides a means for the collaborative construction of what will count as success and thus avoids some predetermined measures of success that may or may not resonate with what is going on in the program.

In this department, the very ability to create an ideal curriculum allowed the faculty to generate the standards by which they would both evaluate students and be evaluated themselves. These issues were difficult ones for the department and had histories that created a great deal of tension within the group. By building on strengths, resources, and ideals, participants felt free to experiment with the process of evaluation (which they are currently doing). The notion that there had to be a preset standard by which to judge their competencies as teachers or the competencies of their students was at least temporarily suspended. This suspension has allowed a continual creativity to circulate within the department. This is not to suggest that the determination of criteria for assessment is never appropriate. Rather, as this faculty works through the conversation about their curriculum and their working relations, the acceptance of fluid, evolving criteria appears to be more generative. Finally, it is important to note that appreciatively oriented evaluation is not devoid of judgments. Rather, it invites judgment of what is happening within a frame of what works best or how to experience more successes. In sum, this case is suggestive of the potential for appreciative evaluation to enhance program improvement by virtue of the different conversations it invites among program participants.

Appendix: The Ideal Curriculum for the Writing Program

I. Philosophy: The Department is committed to the following: Risk taking, originality, ambition, imagination
  A. Core Commitments
    1. In teaching
      a. All genres/all ages
      b. Process, continuity, patience
      c. "The teaching of writing document"
      d. Build continuity of courses
      e. Student-centered (meeting students where they are)
      f. Individual attention
      g. Diversity of methodology, flexibility, autonomy
      h. Exposure to different genres and modes at each level
      i. Appreciation for the uniqueness of pedagogy's own calendar
      j. Extensive feedback
    2. In students' works
      a. Writing efficiently to deadline
      b. Writing for self-knowledge
      c. Writing as habit of discovery, thinking
      d. Writing every day
      e. Growth is greater than grades
      f. Reflection
      g. Engage in process
      h. Sensitivity to audience, communication skills and strategies
II. Elements of the Curriculum
  A. Necessary elements
    1. Related to classroom management
      a. Portion of class time devoted to writing
      b. Individual attention
      c. Time for conferences
      d. Frequency of writing and feedback (more time for both)
      e. Timeliness of feedback
      f. Flexibility
      g. Provide models
      h. Writing intensive courses
    2. Related to students' skill acquisition
      a. Thoughtful editing
      b. Revision
      c. Subtle skill (word choice, organic source, metaphor)
      d. Various modes of expression

        e. Seeing
        f. Audience
        g. Voice
        h. Versatility
     3. Related to students' assignments
        a. Writing and prewriting
        b. Portfolio, exhibition
  B. Useful elements
     1. Poetry collection
     2. Meditation
III. Structure of Curriculum
  A. Related to classroom management
     1. Ample time for conferences with students
     2. Three sections per teacher
     3. A list of writing assignments similar to the list of texts
     4. Service-learning
     5. Additional writing elective available all terms
     6. Develop writing course
  B. Related to resources that would enhance teaching
     1. Use of computer/writing center
     2. Senior tutors of others in a writing center
  C. Related to the school and department structure
     1. Time to get papers back in a week
     2. Fewer students (perhaps fewer class meetings?)
     3. One-week block modules (not Saturday) of ninety minutes to two hours
     4. Longer format, class periods
     5. Different structure for senior year
     6. Lighter load for some teachers (for example, to fill in for illness)
     7. Writing course teachers teach a lighter load
     8. Free weekends
  D. Related to assignments and grading
     1. Written assessment, not letter grades
     2. Variety of work
     3. Senior project with evaluations
IV. Remaining Questions and Issues
  A. Curricular goals of the department
     1. To teach students in the following genres:
        a. Analysis
        b. Exposition
        c. Narration
           i. Need a conversation about what we mean by "narrative"
          ii. Narrative as a set of rules versus narrative as consistent with student-centered pedagogy
         iii. Role of narrative (writing in their own voice) in all forms of writing

        iv. Is narrative a "foundation to build on" or a "formula to be true to"
        v. Discuss "old guard" and "new guard" views on the meaning of narrative
    2. To refine students' skills in grammar and mechanics, structure
    3. To clearly define our program
  B. Consequences of teacher autonomy
    1. What do we mean when we say we value autonomy?
      a. There is a huge level of trust
      b. What do we lose or what could we lose in our celebration of autonomy?
        i. Students experience moving through department as arbitrary—no sense that they will need what they learn in future classes
        ii. no consistent set of signals as to what is important
      c. What do we gain in our celebration of autonomy?
        i. Some focus on nuts and bolts
        ii. Some focus on content
        iii. Some focus on style
      d. Each of our ways of teaching may give students new options—not formulaic but authentic ways of approaching writing—gives them more choices
      e. Perhaps we do not articulate our expectations clearly enough for the students
  C. Issues of time
    1. Our need for teaching time
    2. Students' needs for writing process time
  D. Vocabulary issues
    1. Need to articulate to students what they are learning using some common terminology
  E. Respect for professionalism
    1. Trust that we meet students where they are, attend to their needs at whatever level

References

Gergen, K. J. *An Invitation to Social Construction.* Thousand Oaks, Calif.: Sage, 1999.

McNamee, S., and Gergen, K. J. *Relational Responsibility: Resources for Sustainable Dialogue.* Thousand Oaks, Calif.: Sage, 1999.

Sampson, E. E. *Celebrating the Other.* Boulder, Colo.: Westview Press, 1993.

SHEILA MCNAMEE is professor of communication at the University of New Hampshire and holds the university's Class of 1944 Professorship.

3

This chapter describes how Appreciative Inquiry methods were used to focus the evaluation of an international nonprofit organization's Africa-based center, develop interview guides and a questionnaire, engender trust, and maximize utilization of results.

Using Appreciative Inquiry to Guide an Evaluation of the International Women's Media Foundation Africa Program

Tessie Tzavaras Catsambas, Laverne D. Webb

The International Women's Media Foundation (IWMF), established in 1990 in Washington, D.C., to strengthen the role of women in the news media around the world, contracted with EnCompass LLC (an evaluation and training consulting firm serving government, nonprofit, and international organizations) in 2000 to design and implement an evaluation of its three-year-old African Women's Media Center (AWMC), headquartered in Senegal, West Africa.

In 1993, the IWMF hosted a regional conference in Harare, Zimbabwe, which explored women's underrepresentation in executive positions within the African news media. The conference raised a fundamental question: "Will more women in decision-making posts in the media guarantee more equitable and balanced coverage of women's issues?" Four years later, the IWMF established the AWMC in Dakar, Senegal, to build a continent-wide network of professional African women working in the news media. Its purpose was to promote news coverage of issues affecting women and society by supporting women in news media leadership roles, fostering professional networking opportunities, and providing access to education, skills training, and resources.

The IWMF's donor required an evaluation as a condition of continued funding of the media center. The IWMF was concerned that the evaluation process and results have credibility, while ensuring that the evaluators remained sensitive to the organization's needs and realities. Through the evaluation process, the IWMF also sought to learn about the needs and priorities of its constituents to inform an upcoming strategic planning process. Within this context, the IWMF specified that the evaluation was to address the following areas: (1) role, (2) primary objectives and progress in meeting those objectives, (3) organizational leadership, (4) collaborative relationships, and (5) outlook for sustainability.

Evaluation Design and Data Collection Methods

Prior to the IWMF evaluation, EnCompass had been successful in using Appreciative Inquiry as an approach to strategic planning and organization and community change (Poduska, 2001; Webb, 1999) and in adapting Appreciative Inquiry to use in evaluations (Catsambas and others, 2002). Based on these experiences, we proposed using an Appreciative Inquiry approach for the IWMF evaluation. Appreciative Inquiry seemed well suited for this evaluation because the client required a combination of credibility, sensitivity, and honesty and data that would be useful in designing the future of the program. Specifically, the IWMF executive director wanted to evaluate whether the AWMC was working effectively toward the goals the IWMF had set out in creating the center, whether the AWMC was reaching the people it needed to reach, and if its programs were meeting the needs of African women journalists.

Another reason for choosing to use Appreciative Inquiry was the compatibility of its asset-based and participatory approach with the AWMC's overall purpose, structure, and programs. We also believed that the appreciative interview process, which is based on storytelling, was especially applicable in the context of African culture because of its oral history traditions (Catsambas and others, 2002; Odell, 2002).

The IWMF executive director was concerned that incorporating Appreciative Inquiry into the evaluation might be "amorphous . . . and a little soft," but she had just completed a week-long leadership program that focused on building from personal strengths. As a result, she was receptive to the idea of focusing the evaluation on discovering the center's successes. In addition, she believed that learning the perceptions of the AWMC participants and stakeholders was the best way to determine how well the center was working. For these various reasons, an evaluation process that emphasized participation, dialogue, and discovery of best practices appealed to her.

Using Appreciative Inquiry. When designing the IWMF evaluation, we used Appreciative Inquiry to help focus the evaluation, as well as to develop and implement several data collection methods. Specifically, we used Appreciative Inquiry processes to

• Focus the evaluation and develop the evaluation questions.

- Design and conduct appreciative individual and group interviews with AWMC members, AWMC advisory committee members, collaborators, and IWMF and AWMC staff.
- Design and implement an appreciative questionnaire.
- Synthesize results and prepare the evaluation report.

In addition, the selected methods were intended to:

- Obtain, document, celebrate, and disseminate program successes and best practices.
- Foster in-depth dialogue and reflection among different stakeholders, including members, leadership, management, and collaborators.
- Reach and actively engage as many as possible of AWMC's members and the leadership of both the AWMC and IWMF.
- Engage the AWMC in interactive, whole-systems learning.

When conducting the evaluation, we followed the 4-I model of Appreciative Inquiry as explained in Chapter One.

Focusing the Evaluation. To develop the evaluation's guiding questions and focus of the evaluation, we conducted a four-hour Appreciative Inquiry process with the executive director, key staff, and board chair. These participants interviewed one another, using the following adapted version of the generic appreciative protocol presented in Chapter One:

1. Reflect for a moment on your involvement with the Africa Program over the last three years, and remember a high point or peak experience—a time when you were most proud and fulfilled to be a member of the IWMF and the AWMC program. Tell the story. What happened? What made this peak experience possible? Who else was important in making this experience happen?
2. What do you most value about yourself? Your work at IWMF/AWMC?
3. If you had three wishes to make more of these peak experiences possible, what would they be?

After completing the interviews, the group shared their stories and determined the key themes, core values, and top wishes for the future. They then responded to the question, "What questions should the evaluation answer?" Members individually identified priorities for the evaluation based on the data from the stories. Participants jotted down their ideas on sticky notes, which they displayed on the wall. Together, they organized the notes into key categories or questions for the evaluation. The evaluation questions covered four areas: training programs, networking, support and resource materials, and organization and management. Participants then identified key stakeholder groups and individuals within each group as the intended users of the evaluation findings. From these lists of questions, key categories, and stakeholders, EnCompass developed and submitted an evaluation plan to the IWMF, proposing evaluation questions, corresponding indicators, information sources, and data collection methods.

Conducting Appreciative Interviews. After developing the evaluation plan, the IWMF held an international conference that brought the African AWMC advisory committee members to Washington. The advisory committee had been established in 1997 to help guide the IWMF start-up phase. The committee was made up of women journalists from throughout Africa and from the United States and chaired by Judy Woodruff of CNN and Elizabeth Ohene of the BBC, both members of the board of directors of the IWMF.

At this conference, we conducted a day-long Appreciative Inquiry session with sixteen current and prospective AWMC advisory committee members to collect information on "the best" of the AWMC. Using the appreciative protocol designed earlier with AWMC key staff, participants conducted appreciative interviews in pairs. As a large group, participants then shared each other's stories, values, and wishes and identified common themes. Participants then conducted the Imagine phase, which included crafting provocative propositions or possibility statements.

Engaging the African advisory committee members in this phase of data collection posed an important challenge. The members were at first concerned about and reluctant to expose their thoughts publicly. To put them at ease, we presented some key Appreciative Inquiry principles and invited them to the "higher calling" of not just evaluating the AWMC but helping to shape the future of the organization. As a result, most members overcame the fear of "biting the hand that feeds you" and participated fully. This Appreciative Inquiry process generated useful information regarding the value of AWMC's programs and key organizational issues for its evolution and sustainability.

Following the Appreciative Inquiry interviews with the AWMC Advisory Committee, we conducted fourteen appreciative interviews with other key stakeholders (to address the evaluation questions), such as board members, African media members, academic and nongovernmental organization representatives, and U.S. government personnel, using the following questions, which explored the role and unique niche of the AWMC in supporting African women in media:

1. What is the nature of your collaboration with the AWMC?
2. What is the single greatest contribution the AWMC has made to women in media in Africa?
3. What does the AWMC offer that other similar media organizations do not?
4. What other organizations work to support women in the media? What do they do? How are they different from AWMC?
5. What needs of women in the media are not addressed by any organization?

6. What do you most value about the AWMC?
7. What three wishes would you have for AWMC that would enable it to make even greater contributions to women in media in Africa in the future?

EnCompass conducted these interviews by telephone when possible and over the Internet and by fax when telephone contact was not successful.

Implementing an Appreciative Questionnaire. EnCompass developed an appreciative questionnaire, which was translated into French for Francophone members, and distributed it to all members through mail, e-mail, or fax, as well as posted on the Internet. The questions had been tested and revised in the Appreciative Inquiry session with the AWMC advisory committee. This questionnaire sought feedback through a series of appreciative questions (two of them are presented as examples in Exhibit 3.1).

The questionnaire was mailed to 650 people throughout Africa and was posted on the organization's Web site. However, mail is often slow and unreliable in parts of Africa, and there was no way to know if the questionnaire ever reached the intended respondents. As for e-mail, many people can access it only by going to a cybercafé or by sharing a computer with others. And because getting on-line can be expensive, e-mail is often accessed

Exhibit 3.1. Sample Appreciative Questions from the AWMC Questionnaire

5. My best experience(s) with the AWMC have been in the area(s) of (mark as many as apply)
   ❑ Skills training
   ❑ Using the Web site
   ❑ On the Wire (newsletter)
   ❑ The cyberconference
   ❑ Carole Simpson Leadership Institute
   ❑ Handbook for Media Leadership
   ❑ Resource Directory for Women Journalists
   ❑ Networking
   ❑ Other _____

6. The aspects of AWMC that are most important to me are (mark as many as apply)
   ❑ AWMC programs are organized well and run smoothly.
   ❑ The topics covered are critical for African women in the media.
   ❑ The wonderful and inspiring stories from other women.
   ❑ Meeting people who became important in my life and work.
   ❑ I learned new skills.
   ❑ I learned about reporting on current issues.
   ❑ I became aware of useful resources.
   ❑ I became connected to other women in the media.
   ❑ I gained respect and stature in my work.
   ❑ I received reinforcement of my power through exposure to other women leaders.
   ❑ Other _____

only intermittently. As a result, we received only forty-four completed questionnaires, despite our efforts over a two-month period to increase the response rate. Although the results of the questionnaire cannot be generalized to the entire membership, they may suggest areas of interest.

Preparing the Evaluation Report. EnCompass consolidated and presented both the quantitative and qualitative results from the data collection in a final evaluation report to the IWMF. Rather than organizing the report by the evaluation's key questions, we described the Appreciative Inquiry applications and their related findings. The findings thus addressed the AWMC's role, progress in meeting its primary objectives, membership, organizational leadership, collaborative relationships, and outlook for sustainability. In doing so, we answered the various evaluation questions and generated numerous recommendations.

Evaluation Findings

At the start of the evaluation, the IWMF was concerned that the AWMC had not accomplished as much as was intended. Yet as the evaluation proceeded, the IWMF was surprised to learn all that the center had actually achieved—for example:

• *The AWMC's role.* The evaluation confirmed the AWMC's unique role in offering African women journalists training and access in traditionally male arenas. For example, all forty-four respondents indicated that the AWMC plays a unique and very important role for African women journalists.

• *Programs.* Responses from AWMC members suggest that AWMC programs were meeting member needs in ways that were not being met otherwise. When asked to identify the most important aspects of AWMC's programs (see Exhibit 3.1, question 6), the top four responses were training, empowerment, promoting opportunities for women, and networking. In response to a question about the most important topics for training that the AWMC should offer, respondents reported Internet use and research and HIV/AIDS prevention.

• *Networking.* Members identified networking as AWMC's key priority now and in the future. In looking ahead, members requested cross-country exchanges, mentoring opportunities, and opportunities to include men in AWMC programs.

• *Sustainability.* Impressively, the AWMC had become a registered nongovernmental organization in just three years, a complicated process in Senegal that often takes much longer to achieve. Registration is an important aspect of credibility in Africa and, thus, of sustainability. Furthermore, since its launch in 1997, AWMC's membership had grown to 648 individuals.

• *Leadership and empowerment.* As a result of the way in which data were collected and specifically how questions were asked, a certain amount of trust developed between the evaluation team and AWMC. This strengthened AWMC members' ability and willingness to discuss and address some of the serious issues that arose in the evaluation related to leadership and empowerment.

Prior to the evaluation and as the AWMC evolved, African advisory committee members had struggled to define their role within the organization. The appreciative interviews gave them an opportunity to address their concerns, develop ideas and plans for a higher level of activity and expansion of their role, and reach a deeper level of commitment to the future. The evaluation data further revealed controversial issues, such as the desire for African leadership of AWMC and the need for clarity about the roles and responsibilities of the advisory committee members. Evaluation data also revealed specific operational issues such as the limitations of the Web site, difficulties in evaluating training, and challenges of sustainability.

Evaluation Results: Two Years Later

EnCompass requested a postevaluation review by IWMF staff in August 2002. The IWMF executive director, program director, director of operations and Web strategies, and project manager for the AWMC, all key staff engaged in the initial evaluation, met independently of EnCompass to respond to the following series of questions about the effects of using an Appreciative Inquiry approach and methods in the IWMF and AWMC evaluation:

1. What factors led you to select the appreciative evaluation approach and methods proposed for the evaluation by EnCompass?
2. How did this "appreciative evaluation" differ from other evaluations you have experienced? What did you most value? What most concerned you about this appreciative approach to evaluation—in the beginning and at the end?
3. How did you experience the role of the evaluators? Did this role affect the outcome of the evaluation in any way? Please discuss and describe.
4. In what ways did the "appreciative evaluation" methods obscure, minimize, reveal, or address problems and issues? Please discuss and describe.
5. This evaluation was conducted in a very diverse cultural setting. How did the appreciative methods used in the evaluation address cultural diversity? What impact did the appreciative methods have on the client population and beneficiaries of services of the AWMC?
6. What impact, if any, has this evaluation had on the IWMF and AWMC? Please describe.

The IWMF's general response stated that both the evaluation process and results enabled them to address specific and significant challenges. For example, the IWMF reported that the controversial issue of African leadership was fully addressed and resolved following the evaluation:

> Since the evaluation took place, we have made some dramatic changes in the leadership of the organization. It had always been the goal to transition the AWMC to a more Africa-based and Africa-led autonomous organization. The evaluation results reinforced that goal and perhaps moved us in that direction more quickly than we would have otherwise gone. . . . At the time of the evaluation the AWMC had an American director, an advisory committee made up of Americans and Africans and was chaired by an American and an African living in London. Since the evaluation a new director has been hired—a journalist from The Gambia with 25 years of experience in radio and a background in leading NGOs in Africa [Rockey, 2002].

Another critical issue identified in the evaluation was the need to strengthen the roles and responsibilities of the African advisory committee. The IWMF reported that as a result of the evaluation, this issue also was resolved successfully:

> The advisory committee, which was not particularly effective, was disbanded. A new vision for the advisory committee was developed by an African IWMF board member and the new African AWMC director. The new advisory committee is organized with the intent of creating a governing board and is made up of only Africans. . . . The advisory committee met in January 2002 to develop a mission, vision and strategic plan for the AWMC. While the IWMF continues to be a primary source of resource development for the AWMC, the director has significant authority to move the organization forward in new ways [Rockey, 2002].

Since the evaluation, the IWMF has found that senior staff often incorporate elements of Appreciative Inquiry in their evaluation work. For example, staff members are asking questions differently than they did in the past, now with a deliberate focus on how to improve, grow, and learn from their successes. Members report:

> In working with the IWMF board of directors we are planning to develop a mechanism for them to evaluate IWMF programs in general and believe that the "appreciative evaluation" method will be a productive way to do this. It's too easy for a board discussion to focus on the negative and on minutia and we plan to use an "appreciative evaluation" method to keep them on the big picture and ensure that the effort flows into the strategic planning process [Rockey, 2002].

Finally, the IWMF staff explored the dynamic of the Appreciative Inquiry interview and dialogue process, drawing some interesting conclusions:

I believe that because the process emphasizes values and experiences, it allows for people engaged together in the process to form important personal bonds. It helps to expose cultural differences in how we all might relate to an organization and its services. It creates relationships and therefore a safe place and a comfortable place from which to make critique [Rockey, 2002].

Issues in Using Appreciative Inquiry in Evaluation

In conducting this and similar evaluations, EnCompass has encountered two types of challenges in adapting Appreciative Inquiry to evaluation: those perceived by people who are not familiar with Appreciative Inquiry and those experienced by practitioners incorporating Appreciative Inquiry into their evaluation work.

Perceived Challenges. When EnCompass presents its use of Appreciative Inquiry in evaluation, some questions regularly arise:

• *Does the positive bias seemingly inherent in Appreciative Inquiry get in the way of honesty and neutrality?* In response to the question, "In what ways did the appreciative evaluation methods obscure, minimize, reveal, or address problems and issues?" the IWMF discussed whether there is an inherent positive bias in using Appreciative Inquiry in evaluation. The IWMF explained, "Yes, but the bias did not affect the outcome. Our goal in conducting the evaluation was to look at the big picture and to move toward the future. The bias did not prevent us from feeling that the organization was able to make a fair assessment of how to do that" [Rockey, 2002].

From our perspective, all evaluators are inherently "biased" based on their own backgrounds, values, experiences, and expectations. Because evaluation and organizational development processes are interventions, evaluators have a responsibility to be concerned about the effect they have on the systems they are entering.

• *What about the problems? Are they hidden from the evaluator's keen eye by the "positive cloud" of Appreciative Inquiry?* A related issue is how problems are identified and how organizations can change if they do not address their problems. The IWMF provides some important insights into this issue:

The "problems" are dealt with in a more implicit way. By discussing effectiveness and success, the elements that do not fall into those categories become apparent through a natural selection process. The "wishes" approach brings critique in through the back door. The question is structured positively—i.e., "how can we strengthen, what do we want to see in the future." In that way the participants can address critiques from a productive standpoint, without blame and defensiveness. Instead of responding that it is wrong to not have Africa leadership the response becomes "our wish is to move toward more African leadership in the future." The critique is in there. The wish to do something different in the future is the critique. It's not necessary to call it a "problem" [Rockey, 2002].

As seen in this case, using Appreciative Inquiry raised problems quickly and honestly. This is because of both the increased trust Appreciative Inquiry creates and the freedom it gives to people to speak in appreciative ways or to, for example, state issues as "wishes" rather than as "problems."

• *Do clients resist engaging in evaluations that use Appreciative Inquiry because they do not think it is a credible approach?* EnCompass typically weaves Appreciative Inquiry approaches and methods into its evaluation design and work as appropriate to the situation, often without drawing specific attention to the methods. When questions arise about a particular application of Appreciative Inquiry in evaluation, the client's questions are answered. The goal here is to use Appreciative Inquiry processes in evaluation to increase trust, participation, and learning and to help the client change according to the lessons learned. In the case of the AWMC, the use of Appreciative Inquiry processes in the evaluation was explicitly presented. The IWMF ultimately embraced the Appreciative Inquiry approach and developed its organizational capacity for continued appreciative reflection and motivation.

• *What are the limitations of Appreciative Inquiry, and when is it appropriate to use it?* In terms of the limitations of Appreciative Inquiry in evaluation, Appreciative Inquiry is simply one of numerous methods for developing evaluation questions, designing and conducting individual and group interviews, identifying indicators, and designing and conducting focus group discussions. There are circumstances that are appropriate for using Appreciative Inquiry and others that are not. Organizations that embrace evaluation as a process for learning and organizational change are good candidates for this approach. Evaluations that aim to close or terminate nonfunctioning programs may find Appreciative Inquiry approaches inappropriate. Appreciative Inquiry may not be an appropriate approach for evaluations that require quantitative data, such as experimental and quasi-experimental studies, although Appreciative Inquiry could be used for developing the evaluation questions and interpreting the results.

Challenges to Practitioners. Evaluators applying Appreciative Inquiry are exploring innovative frontiers and often face new challenges. In using Appreciative Inquiry in the IWMF evaluation, we faced several challenges, including developing good appreciative questions, honing reframing skills, and staying within the boundaries of evaluation.

Developing good appreciative questions is at the heart of Appreciative Inquiry. As with most other evaluation methods, evaluators frequently have to control the urge to manipulate, direct, or lead participants. In addition, staying "appreciative" is difficult for many respondents and evaluators. Most people have had years of experience identifying and analyzing deficits and gaps. Thus, an evaluator using Appreciative Inquiry has to stay alert and keep reframing the conversation to search for the exceptional moments and elements of excellence, and through that path, explore the rest of the system, including its weaknesses and areas for improvement.

Another challenge for the practitioner is that clients who experience the energy and trust that Appreciative Inquiry often generates may want to push the evaluator beyond the usual boundaries of evaluation and into the realm of organizational development and change management. It may be challenging for the evaluator to stay focused on the evaluation task and not to veer away from the original purpose of the evaluation.

Conclusion

Using Appreciative Inquiry in evaluation is not a panacea. As seen in this case, Appreciative Inquiry offers ways of reframing questions for individual and group interviews and questionnaires for obtaining data that will help expand the best there is in an organization or program. It also provides a structured, intensive, and collaborative way of engaging clients and stakeholders in an evaluation and an effective means by which they can tell their stories with their own words. Applying Appreciative Inquiry will not make an organization or program's challenges or problems disappear. Instead, Appreciative Inquiry in evaluation provides another way for drawing out and addressing issues and making evaluation effective and useful to clients, meaningful to other stakeholders and beneficiaries, and supportive of change.

We have found that Appreciative Inquiry helps clients to be honest, more open, and collaborative. We are then able to focus more quickly on key issues and questions. In our experience, using Appreciative Inquiry in evaluation leads to results that clients are more likely to embrace and address even when the evaluation delivers a tough message.

References

Catsambas, T., and others. "The Evaluation of Quality Assurance: Developing and Testing Practical Methods for Managers." *International Journal for Quality and Healthcare,* 2002, *14*(Suppl. 1), 75–81.

Odell, M. *"Beyond the Box": An Innovative Habitat for Humanity Paradigm for Participatory Planning, Monitoring and Evaluation—Measuring and Increasing Program Impacts with Appreciative Inquiry.* Americus, Ga.: Habitat for Humanity International, 2002.

Poduska, J. P. "Dubuque Reforms Administration of Section 8 Voucher Program with Help from Owners, Tenants, Local Groups." *Housing and Development Reporter,* Apr. 2, 2001, pp. 746–748.

Rockey, S. Memorandum to EnCompass, Aug. 2, 2002.

Webb, L. "Appreciative Inquiry as a Way to Jump Start Change." *At Work,* 1999, 8(2), 1–3.

TESSIE TZAVARAS CATSAMBAS is president of EnCompass LLC in Bethesda, Maryland.

LAVERNE D. WEBB is CEO of EnCompass LLC in Bethesda, Maryland.

4

Appreciative Inquiry was used to highlight the successes of a donor-supported project of working with victims of trauma in an environment of civil war and high security risk, and thereby also to honor the work of dedicated staff who often face extremely difficult situations.

Using Appreciative Inquiry to Evaluate Project Activities of a Nongovernmental Organization Supporting Victims of Trauma in Sri Lanka

Mette Jacobsgaard

The Family Rehabilitation Center (FRC) in Sri Lanka is a nongovernmental, humanitarian, nonprofit service organization that was established in 1992 to provide island-wide care for those affected by armed conflict. Its main objective is to identify and meet the psychological and medical needs of victims of torture, as well as serve their immediate relatives. In addition to health-related activities, FRC supports activities that contribute to the prevention of torture.

At the time of the evaluation discussed in this chapter, FRC operated within the context of a country that had been in a state of civil war and emergency for thirty years. This meant that crisis regulations and special laws were in force, and state impunity was accorded to members of the security forces who committed grave human rights violations. The war between the government of Sri Lanka and the Liberation Tigers of Tamil Elam, especially in the North and the East, created a situation where large areas were outside government control and therefore largely inaccessible to

The author thanks A. S. Poovendran, acting executive director and chairman, Senior Management Committee/Project Coordinator, Family Rehabilitation Center, Sri Lanka, for kindly providing information about the evaluation's impact and the effect of using Appreciative Inquiry.

53

FRC staff. Human rights violations and violations of humanitarian law were reported on a large scale in Sri Lanka in the context of the civil war, which increasingly polarized factions along ethnic lines. Amnesty International's report from 1998 stated that "thousands of Tamil people were arrested, including scores of possible prisoners of conscience. Torture and ill-treatment in army and police custody were widespread and people have disappeared. A more recent report released by the Bureau of Democracy, Human Rights and Labor of the U.S. Department of State (2001) gives a well-documented account of political and extrajudicial killing; disappearances; torture and other cruel, inhuman, and degrading treatment or punishment; arbitrary arrests, detention, or exile; denial of fair public trial; and so on.

FRC, which is staffed by doctors, nurses, physiotherapists, pharmacists, counselors, and psychologists, is equipped to deal with the health-related symptoms and the effects of armed conflict through the provision of health care, physiotherapy, and psychological counseling. As a health-based and nonpolitical organization, FRC has managed to cross lines of control to provide assistance to all groups regardless of ethnic origin.

The Family Rehabilitation Center's Goals, Objectives, and Activities

FRC has formed a partnership with the Danish Rehabilitation and Research Center for Torture Victims (RCT) in Copenhagen. RCT supports FRC financially through bilateral funding from the Danish government. In addition, it provides FRC staff with skills and supervision training in their respective fields, including physiotherapy and psychotherapy, as well as prevention. The prevention activities typically focus on raising awareness about the effects of torture and to some extent campaigns against torture. FRC receives funding from RCT on the basis of a project proposal and a mutually agreed project document that describes the project's objectives, activities, and expected outputs. According to the agreement between the Danish government and RCT, a midterm evaluation of the activities that are being funded should be carried out on a regular basis.

The project's long-term objective is to reduce the practice of torture and to make Sri Lanka's public and the national health system aware of the needs of victims of torture and severe trauma throughout the country. The project's short-term objectives are to (1) identify, treat, and rehabilitate a minimum of four thousand torture and trauma victims, (2) enhance the professional skills of FRC staff, (3) train health professionals how to serve victims of torture, and (4) influence the attitudes of law enforcement and opinion makers.

In order to achieve the project's objectives, it is vital to reach victims of torture and trauma in a systematic and organized manner. To facilitate this, the country is divided into four zones, each with a number of outreach centers from which FRC operates, though FRC maintains its headquarters in the capital, Colombo. The project planning document lists a number of activities that were expected to achieve the stated objectives. These include identifying and training doctors at local hospitals, training field officers and hiring more trained counselors for the outreach centers, initiating discussions with the training school authority and Ministry of Defence to establish a working arrangement, and conducting awareness programs.

Activities are usually planned with the assumption that events can be reasonably predicted. For example, one activity is to "initiate discussions with the training school authority and Ministry of Defence to establish a working arrangement." Some assumptions made are that this working arrangement can be established, that it is going to produce an output (in this case, a level of awareness that will ultimately lead to the prevention of torture), and that the regime and attitude of the Ministry of Defence will not change during the project period. This last assumption was somewhat tenuous given the civil war situation at the time, because the Ministry of Defence would need to react accordingly to any unexpected security situations. Given the fact that FRC is committed to giving island-wide service to all victims of torture and trauma, regardless of ethnic origin and political alliance, it also treats clients on the border of government-controlled lines and sometimes within these.

FRC staff often risk their lives to assist the target group, because the security situation in Sri Lanka often changes dramatically with little advance notice, and the perpetrators are often security personnel and government employees. Therefore, plans for activities one day—perhaps to visit an outreach center or carry out physiotherapy training at an outreach center—could easily be rendered infeasible or impossible the following day. This uncertainty existed in regard to the activities that were described in the project document. The original plan was to sensitize senior officials, security personnel, and the judiciary to the issue of torture. However, the planned activities turned out to be far too sensitive for these discussions to take place; working directly with the Ministry of Defence would have heightened the profile of FRC's work and possibly therefore threatened other FRC activities. FRC found alternative ways to achieve this objective, which included sensitizing lower-grade officers through the FRC outreach centers. As a result of this dynamic and often unpredictable context, FRC had rolling contingency plans that at times did not match the activities stated in the project document. Nevertheless, FRC staff believed that these modified activities still contributed toward achieving the established objectives.

Evaluating the Family Rehabilitation Center's Work

The evaluation of FRC's activities under the project funded by Danida, the Danish government aid agency, was carried out in Sri Lanka in April 2001 as part of a larger evaluation of Danida assistance to RCT and its partners

(FRC was one out of eleven partners). The evaluation was to assess the project's progress and results against the objectives set forth in the project document and to assess FRC's capacity to implement the project. The evaluators were asked to include as part of the evaluation observations and assessments of FRC's strategic approach, networking activities, participation methodologies, and how it was working with its local partners.

RCT believed that FRC's efforts should be viewed as a pilot project, and as such any evaluation should capture the nuances and context of the project's implementation. Thus, while they would strive to determine the extent to which the project's objectives were being met, they were also interested in looking beyond attainment of the objectives, especially given the unpredictable environment in which FRC operated. Balancing this view with the fact that Danida wanted to see progress measured against what was outlined in the project document, the evaluators sought an evaluation approach that would serve both purposes.

Previous Evaluations of the Family Rehabilitation Center. Evaluations of development aid projects, including a previous evaluation of the FRC, typically begin with evaluators reviewing project plans and site reports. These reports tend to focus on a project's deficits or problems and result in a list of recommendations for remedying the identified problems. The underlying assumption has been that if the evaluation can uncover problems and identify and recommend solutions, then the project's objectives will be attained. Consequently, most evaluations take a deficit-based approach in both their design and implementation.

As the FRC staff faced another evaluation, they were somewhat apprehensive. First, they were concerned about being evaluated by outsiders whom they had never met and who knew little about the organization, its staff, and its operational capacity. Second, the fact that FRC staff assumed that they would be evaluated on the basis of the activities stated in the project document added to this uneasiness. Third, FRC had just months prior to the evaluation been visited by an RCT representative who had been critical of the project's seeming lack of progress in certain areas. The RCT's report (2001) concluded, "The organisation (FRC) had failed to implement the planned activities (with respect to prevention) in the years 1999 and 2000." The report also mentioned a number of recommendations that FRC should follow but that the staff believed were difficult to comply with due to their working environment. Understandably, the staff's inclination was to be defensive when the subject of this new evaluation came up.

Using Appreciative Inquiry. If the starting point of an evaluation is to look for problems, then problems will certainly be found. In the process of focusing on problems, however, the evaluators may not be able to see areas in which the project has experienced significant success. As explained in Chapter One of this volume, the basic assumption of Appreciative Inquiry is that what worked best in the past is what will carry an organization forward. Thus, Appreciative Inquiry does not dwell on what has not been done, but instead focuses on areas in which the organization has succeeded. Appreciative Inquiry is a way of thinking, a way of understanding the world as a place of opportunities rather than intractable problems. Therefore, it was considered a particularly appropriate evaluation approach for an organization like FRC, which operates in a volatile environment and could be seen as riddled with problems (as previous evaluation reports had highlighted). Taking an Appreciative Inquiry approach to evaluation also starts with the supposition that the organization's members are most knowledgeable about their work and therefore best able to evaluate the effectiveness of their own activities. As a result, the evaluation is highly participative and process oriented.

In the case of FRC, Appreciative Inquiry was chosen as the evaluation approach for several reasons. First, we believed that taking this approach would honor FRC's innovative attempts to meet the project's objectives even though its approaches were different from those stated in the project document. Second, previous FRC evaluations that had used a problem-focused approach resulted in a list of problems and recommendations to solve the problems. The staff strongly believed that these evaluations failed to capture the unstable and challenging conditions in which FRC operates—an environment of civil war with victims of torture. Moreover, these previous evaluations did not consider the horror of the everyday work life of FRC staff. Third, using an Appreciative Inquiry approach would take into account the fact that frequent changes of plans had to be accommodated. Frequently operating within the context of suspicion between different population groups, armed conflict, and the real possibility of terrorist attacks meant that FRC often had to change plans at a moment's notice. Thus, it made sense to find out where and how FRC was successful despite the incredible odds. Although neither RCT nor Danida indicated or required the use of Appreciative Inquiry as the evaluation approach, they did express openness to participatory methods and Appreciative Inquiry during the contract negotiations.

Evaluation Design and Implementation. If Appreciative Inquiry were used as the overarching approach to conducting an evaluation it would follow either the 4-D or 4-I cycle described in Chapter One. It first would help to determine the evaluation's focus and key questions and who would be involved in the evaluation process. Then by asking appreciatively worded questions in the Discover phase, the stakeholders would discover "the best of what has been," as well as the hopes and possibilities for the future. Based on these results, the stakeholders would move to the Dream phase about the future based on what was discussed in the discovery phase. The Design phase would illuminate the changes needed to bring the dream to life. Finally, in the Deliver phase, the stakeholders would develop and implement their plans in order to deliver the future they dreamed about.

In the case of FRC, the project's funders (the RCT and Danida) had already determined the evaluation's purpose and focus in the Terms of

Reference (job descriptions), which also dictated that the evaluators were to draft a report that included the evaluation's outcomes. This placed some pressure on the evaluators in terms of ensuring that sufficient information was collected to write the report, while at the same time staying true to the appreciative format and honoring FRC's internal organizational processes.

To conduct the evaluation using an Appreciative Inquiry approach, we carried out the Discovery phase through a number of workshops and small meetings. The reason for this was partly to accommodate the wishes of FRC and partly for practical reasons. FRC and RCT had proposed that a number of stakeholders be included in the evaluation. FRC had also scheduled meetings with these stakeholders prior to the arrival of the evaluators, and some of the stakeholders, in turn, expected us (the evaluators) to participate in their meetings.

A one-day workshop was also organized with FRC staff during which the appreciatively worded questions were asked, stories told, and themes listed from the stories. In addition, we held small group half-day discussions with FRC staff, during which they discussed specific work activities. The themes from their stories were also identified and listed. Staff at some of the outreach centers were interviewed as a group by the evaluators through FRC translators. The clients who happened to visit the outreach center that day were also interviewed. A couple of meetings with other stakeholders provided additional data. These stakeholders included clients of FRC and staff members of the prison service, the teaching hospital, the Human Rights Commission, and other nongovernmental organizations.

The group meetings and workshops varied in length and number of participants. The largest group was the workshop with Colombo-based FRC staff, in addition to a few staff members from the outreach centers. The following are examples of the generative questions we asked in the meetings and interviews. Which questions we asked depended on whether the interviews were with internal FRC staff or with external stakeholders:

FRC Staff
• When did the staff, board, and others believe that FRC was at its best?
• What excites you the most about working for FRC?
• When had the support from RCT been at its best?
• What was most appreciated by the partnership with RCT?
• Tell us about a time when clients responded really positively to FRC's work.
• What are the wishes that you have for FRC?
• Tell us about situations when you (FRC) have been most successful in prevention of torture and violence.
• Talk about a situation when all staff capacity in FRC was involved in successfully moving a case.

External Stakeholders
- What was it about the service provided by FRC that the clients and/or the government most appreciated?
- Tell us how FRC contributes positively to the work of your organization.
- Tell us about a situation when you collaborated successfully with FRC.
- What are the wishes that you have for the future work of FRC?

The evaluators typically asked the questions, and anyone in the group who wanted to talk could answer. In other situations, a question was asked of each person in the group—for example, "What excites you the most about working for FRC?"

As is often the case when using an Appreciative Inquiry approach, the atmosphere in the meetings and workshops was relaxed and joyful. All of those interviewed had much to say and appreciated being given the opportunity to tell their stories. Their narratives provided valuable information about how FRC had been innovative in finding ways to conduct training sessions and visit outreach centers despite extreme difficulties. The stories illustrated a great deal of bravery and ingenuity. As noted earlier, the activities listed in the project document for the prevention of torture and increased awareness had been impossible to achieve. Yet the stories told in answer to the question, "Tell us about situations when you (FRC) have been most successful in prevention of torture and violence," clearly showed how FRC had found ways of achieving the original objectives without necessarily sticking to the activities prescribed in the project document.

In the large group interviews with FRC staff, the major themes from the stories were written on flip charts as the stories were being told. This served two purposes: it helped document the stories so they could be remembered, and it generated some excitement in the group when they revisited the themes that came out of their stories. A large amount of information was gathered, all of which was extremely useful for writing the evaluation report. Because the information was contextualized through storytelling, everyone seemed to remember it more easily, and as a result the participants were able to contribute suggestions for how to carry the project further.

FRC staff members were asked to think about the information on the flip charts and to determine their priorities. Revisiting the themes reminded them of their stories, of how they had acted and been successful with regard to their project activities as well as internally in the organization. The stories also provided valuable feedback to the RCT representative who was in attendance about times when the partnership with RCT had been at its best and was most appreciated. There were examples of exchange visits between FRC and other RCT partner projects elsewhere in Asia and Africa that had been particularly helpful. FRC wanted to increase such exchanges and structure them better to their and other partners' benefit. It also reminded them that even though problems were present, success was also possible.

For example, participants realized that a large number of activities had in fact been carried out with regard to prevention and increased awareness. Because the earlier RCT evaluation report had concluded that no activities had been implemented as listed in the project document, staff members had almost forgotten that they had succeeded in carrying out a number of other activities.

With a focus on the strengths and possibilities of the past, the FRC staff group came together with the evaluators to dream about the future. The themes generated from their stories were posted on the walls of the meeting room. Additional themes from the stakeholder meetings were added to those generated by the FRC staff group's first meeting. The themes from the group interviews and stakeholder meetings added an important perspective to the themes generated by the FRC staff group. They were categorized according to whether they were organizational and management issues or related to the project's activities. The group then developed provocative propositions or vision statements for the future of FRC.

Evaluation Findings. Taking an Appreciative Inquiry approach to the FRC's project evaluation appeared to work well on several different levels. First, it defused a possible tension among the FRC staff who expected the evaluation to focus on where they had failed, as they had experienced in previous evaluations. Thus, by focusing on what had worked well and why it had worked, the staff were more willing to tell their stories. For example, when focusing on times that the organization's management had been most supportive, several sensitive issues came to the light with regard to a few individuals who were perceived as not performing well. Instead of singling out and blaming these individuals, ideas and wishes for alternative behaviors were identified in a constructive rather than destructive manner. In another example, with regard to funding different FRC efforts, the staff wished for greater flexibility in the quick disbursement of funds when they need to react to emergencies, such as a bomb blast when individuals require immediate attention. From the accountant's perspective, it became clear that his goal was to make sure the funds were in the budget so that they would be available when needed. As the staff told their stories, they came to understand how the organization's activities were prioritized, as well as how they were perceived by other staff members.

Second, the information gathered was extensive, uncensored, and rich in detail. Talking about successful situations, some of which had required rather daring moves with regard to dealing with security forces, brought about laughter and camaraderie. For example, one person told a story about having to deal with security forces at a checkpoint. The security forces had refused to let an FRC client pass through. The client was Tamil and spoke no Singhalese. When the FRC staff later visited this checkpoint, they found that the officers to whom this client had spoken did not speak Tamil. The FRC staff were able to determine that the refusal was based mostly on problems of language and misunderstanding rather than from a possible security risk. From this story, FRC staff learned that they needed to sensitize the security staff by using language problems as examples of situations they might encounter. Other stories highlighted the fact that clients view the outreach centers not only as a place to receive treatment but also as a place to meet other victims of torture and as an entry point into the local community.

In the end, we believe that the data collected using appreciatively oriented questions contributed to a more comprehensive understanding of FRC's activities. The stories people told provided deeper insights into the work and life of the FRC staff than we would have likely obtained through more problem-focused interviews.

Conclusion

The last two phases of the 4-D cycle, Design and Delivery, were left to FRC to carry out. The evaluators wished they could have helped the FRC staff through these phases so that the results could have been embedded into the FRC organization more deliberately. However, the focus of the evaluation was to understand which FRC activities funded by Danida were working particularly well. The evaluators had facilitated a process where a very large amount of useful information had been gathered through the Discovery phase. This information was used in the Dream phase to develop provocative propositions for FRC that served as ideas for recommendations in the evaluation report. Knowing that these ideas were grounded in successes that FRC had had, as well as on participants' wishes and visions, made it much easier for the evaluators to construct meaningful recommendations. In addition, the provocative propositions served as working points for FRC to use when planning and implementing future activities.

When the evaluators asked some of the senior managers to reflect on their experience with the evaluation, and with the Appreciative Inquiry approach in particular, one manager reported:

> The output has increased, a sense of belonging has been created, and duality has been eliminated. What I mean by duality here is how the staff looked at FRC and at themselves. Prior to the evaluation, they looked at FRC as a separate entity and not something belonging to them. Today, they have been inculcated with the spirit of "oneness." In other words, "FRC is they and they are FRC." That is a moment of excellence for me to have integrated their energy and concepts into an inseparable whole. It is an attitudinal change. How to sustain this spirit? The answer lies in how best the future managers will understand and apply Appreciative Inquiry into their line of thinking [A. S. Poovendran, personal communication, 2003].

Reflecting on what he learned from using Appreciative Inquiry for the evaluation, another senior manager noted:

The case study I wish to refer to here is how a laborer level person has been elevated to a procurement clerk. During the past five years I have been studying him. Ever since I have become familiar with the Appreciative Inquiry theory, I wear those glasses and see people. One day I called for his personnel file. I was amazed on one side and dismayed on the other side to observe how this chap was kept as an underdog by the bureaucratic management. His educational qualifications befitted and warranted a better position in FRC. Having seen his curriculum vitae I was convinced that he deserved better treatment. In mid 2002, I put him in charge of procurement. Today, he is in charge of all purchases of materials and equipment required for Colombo and the outreach offices. Before his appointment, corruption was long suspected and the procurement was not streamlined. Today, corruption has been reduced, procurement has been streamlined and the morale of the staff improved when they found management really caring about the staff's future. Moreover, this was a historical milestone in FRC's history, where a lower rank person has been given the opportunity to climb the ladder for a better career purely on merit [A. S. Poovendran, personal communication, 2003].

As I have reflected on this evaluation, I am convinced that the information gathered had very different qualities and was much richer than it would have been had we used a more traditional problem-focused approach to the evaluation and the interview questions. By grounding the wishes and dreams for the future in the staff's stories, they came to own the resulting recommendations that came out of the provocative propositions. I also believe that in the end, the FRC staff had more positive energy to carry their work forward. Building on the knowledge of where and how FRC had succeeded gave them the motivation and creativity to solve the problems that often seemed insurmountable. In fact, one of FRC's senior managers proceeded to take an Appreciative Inquiry training course following the evaluation and has now introduced Appreciative Inquiry as the operational approach in FRC.

References

Amnesty International. *1998 Report: Sri Lanka.* London: Amnesty International, 1998.
Rehabilitation and Research Center for Torture Victims. Copenhagen: Rehabilitation and Research Center for Torture Victims, 2001.
Family Rehabilitation Center Annual Progress Report, 1999–2001. Sri Lanka: Family Rehabilitation Center, 2001.
U.S. Department of State. "Sri Lanka: Country Reports on Human Rights Practices—2000." Washington, D.C.: Government Printing Office, 2001.

METTE JACOBSGAARD, *a founding member of Appreciative Inquiry Consulting, is currently doing research at Cambridge University as well as working as a consultant and trainer.*

5

This chapter presents a case study that used Appreciative Inquiry techniques in conjunction with conventional evaluation methods. It discusses the benefits of using Appreciative Inquiry methods and issues the evaluators encountered.

Incorporating Appreciative Inquiry Methods to Evaluate a Youth Development Program

Dawn Hanson Smart, Mariann Mann

This case study serves as an example of using certain elements of Appreciative Inquiry in conjunction with conventional evaluation methods. In the first two years of the evaluation of Girl Scouts Beyond Bars (GSBB), a scouting program for girls whose mothers are incarcerated, we used conventional data collection methods such as surveys, structured observations, and interviews. In the third year of the evaluation, we incorporated Appreciative Inquiry methods to collect and help analyze additional data. We included Appreciative Inquiry methods to capture more sensitive data on the relationship between program activities and outcomes and to explore whether we could uncover additional indicators to demonstrate program success or areas that needed improvement. We also chose to include Appreciative Inquiry because of its fit with the asset-based scouting program, the evaluation framework, and the participatory evaluation approach. Although we did not use a full application of Appreciative Inquiry, using particular Appreciative Inquiry methods proved to be a valuable addition to the evaluation design by providing a better understanding of what was most meaningful about the program, confirming the program's theory of change and its long-term expected outcomes, and identifying ways to build on the best of what is in the program.

The Girl Scouts Beyond Bars Program

This scouting program serves daughters of women inmates at the Washington Corrections Center for Women (WCCW) and women who are preparing for release at the Tacoma Pre-Release Center (TPR). It is a collaboration begun in 1999 of the WCCW, TPR, and two Girl Scout Councils in western Washington State through funding from the state's Office of Juvenile Justice. The program is based on a national model piloted in the early 1990s and is currently operating in more than thirteen Girl Scout Councils across the United States. The mission and goals of Girl Scouts Beyond Bars (1999) read:

> To extend the values, resources, and programs of Girl Scouting to daughters of women who are incarcerated, in order to break the intergenerational cycle of incarceration. GSBB seeks to accomplish this by providing Girl Scouting opportunities to girls and their mothers:
>
> • To reduce the trauma suffered by the daughter as a result of separation due to her mother's incarceration;
> • To preserve the mother/daughter relationship during the incarceration through enhanced visitation and increased communication; and
> • Ultimately to reduce the likelihood that the daughter will participate in at-risk behaviors by building character, self-confidence, and self-respect through positive role models.

The program's theory of change is that the girls who are involved in it through participation in challenging learning activities with peers, appropriate guidance and emotional support from adults, and the opportunity for increased contact with their mothers will resist engaging in at-risk behavior, including future involvement in crime.

The customary activities long associated with scouting focus on character building. These activities are a part of GSBB, but the heart of the program is building the connection between girls and their mothers. The program combines traditional community-based Girl Scout troop activities and field trips with Corrections Center–based scout meetings involving both mothers and daughters.

The increased visitation between mothers and daughters provides the opportunity for girls to see their mothers in the Corrections Center setting, confirming that their mothers are safe and well and reducing the anxiety of the unknown that children of incarcerated parents often experience. The interaction between mothers and daughters provides the opportunity for them to continue to be a part of one another's lives. The Girl Scout meeting structure also gives mothers the chance to be parental—to provide support, give advice, and perhaps correct behavior. The interaction allows them to retain or rebuild a positive relationship, essential for the child's future. In this regard, research has shown that "the frequency, nature, and duration of parent-child contacts following separation play a critical role in determining a child's future development. . . . In the case of parent-child visitation in jails or prisons, it is clear that this beneficial, low-cost intervention reduces the negative effects of parent-child separation and may also contribute to a reduction of future crime and incarceration among prisoners' children" (Gabel and Johnston, 1995).

During the third year of the evaluation, the GSSB program in Washington served more than eighty girls ranging in age from five to sixteen. The majority of mothers in the program have been incarcerated for less than two years, approximately one-quarter have been at the WCCW for more than five years, and a small number are in prison for life.

Evaluation Design and Data Collection Methods

The Girl Scout Councils were interested not only in accountability to their funder but also in identifying improvements that would increase the chances of program success. In addition, the councils wanted to track progress toward four long-term outcomes they had identified for the program:

- Greater involvement of girls with caring adults
- An increase in girls' positive peer relationships
- An increase in girls' sense of connection to the community
- Preserved and enhanced relationships between girls and their mothers

Short-term and intermediate outcomes chosen for measurement were drawn from two sources. The first source was the developmental assets framework created for youth-related programs (Leffert, Saito, Blyth, and Kroenke, 1996) that has gained popularity in the past decade. This strength-based approach underlies much of today's youth development programming and has advanced the research on youths' progress toward adulthood (Scales and Leffert, 1999). The second source was the work of Connell, Gambone, and Smith (2000) on evaluation of youth development programs. They contend that the availability of support and opportunities, quality of program offerings, and the youths' experience of the program set the stage for achievement of participant outcomes. They believe that evaluations of youth development programs should incorporate these formative and shorter-term outcomes in order to better understand a program's impacts (Connell, Gambone, and Smith, 2000). Decisions on the evaluation design also were made in the light of limited resources and the need to construct an approach that the councils could sustain in the future if outside evaluation resources were no longer available to them.

With these considerations, the evaluation was designed to assess the program model, identify ways to improve program delivery, and track specific outcomes and indicators. These include aspects of the quality of service delivery, the girls' experience in the program, and changes in the girls related to specific developmental assets. The evaluation questions were as follows:

1. Did the program provide opportunities for relationship building that could strengthen the girls' sense of support?
   Did girls receive guidance and practical support from adults?
   Did girls receive emotional support from adults and peers?
   Did mothers and daughters have opportunities to resolve issues related to their mothers' incarceration?
2. Did the program provide opportunities for the girls' meaningful involvement and membership that could strengthen their sense of connection?
   Were girls involved in a mix of interesting activities?
   Were girls involved in making decisions about program activities?
   Was there an increase in girls' sense of belonging?
   Was there an increase in girls' engagement in community service?
3. Did the program provide opportunities for the girls to engage in challenging learning activities that could strengthen their sense of competence?
   Was there improvement in girls' ability to communicate?
   Was there an increase in girls' ability to work with others as part of a group?
   Was there an increase in girls' ability to resolve conflicts?
   Was there an increase in girls' sense of competence?

The overall evaluation design consisted of a mix of qualitative and quantitative data collection methods in each year of the three-year evaluation effort:

- Record review of demographic data on the participating girls and their mothers and meeting description forms completed by Girl Scout leaders after every session held during the year
- Structured observations completed by Girl Scout leaders after each meeting of behaviors and interactions of the girls, among the girls, and between the girls and their mothers
- Written survey of girls, once at the beginning and once at the end of the year
- Written survey of mothers, once at the beginning and once at the end of the year
- Telephone interviews conducted with a sample of girls' guardians at the end of the year

In the third year of the evaluation, Appreciative Inquiry methods were incorporated into the evaluation's design by asking appreciative questions in a focus group interview with girls participating in the program and in a focus group interview and an e-mail questionnaire to Girl Scout leaders.

We decided to use Appreciative Inquiry methods for several reasons. First, Girl Scouting is viewed as an asset-based program designed to cultivate the essential building blocks of girls' development and to build on participants' positive or developmental assets. Appreciative Inquiry is also based on developing the positive aspects of organizations or programs and thus seemed well aligned with GSBB's philosophy. Over the years, we have come to base much of our evaluation practice on the principles of participatory evaluation and have found that program staff are more receptive and more willing to participate in an evaluation that is aligned with their program's culture or philosophy.

Second, we believed that Appreciative Inquiry's focus on identifying the circumstances that make the best possible was congruent with and would add to the overall evaluation design. Helping program stakeholders look behind their stories and personal experience to what they believe was the source of these positive events was in keeping with the construct of the evaluation framework and its attention to the quality of the program and the girls' experience with it. Thus, we sought a design that would reflect the program's theory of change and a means to support and reinforce program outcomes.

Third, since the councils planned to continue GSBB, we believed that the evaluation should clearly identify positive elements of the program. The first two years of the evaluation provided ample evidence of program success and found no major problems in the program's overall theory or its implementation. With this in mind, and knowing that the program was going to continue, we chose to use Appreciative Inquiry methods to help build on what was best about the program.

Application of Appreciative Inquiry Methods

In this multiple method evaluation, we did not conduct a complete Appreciative Inquiry as described in Chapter One, but instead carried out only the Inquire phase of the Appreciative Inquiry process. The lead evaluator met with fourteen of the girls as a part of their Girl Scout meeting and conducted a forty-five-minute appreciative focus group interview. She also conducted a one-hour appreciative focus group interview with four Girl Scout leaders and an appreciative e-mail questionnaire with four leaders who could not attend the group interview.

Both focus groups were conducted with simply an opening explanation about collecting data for the evaluation of the program rather than a formal discussion of Appreciative Inquiry. This was followed by requesting participants to "tell a story or give an example that shows what is best about this Girl Scout troop." After the stories and examples were shared in both focus group interviews, the evaluator asked the girls and the Girl Scout leaders to consider the stories and examples they had just heard and identify themes they thought the stories had in common and the circumstances or conditions that made these "exceptional moments" possible.

Evaluation Findings

In the final evaluation report, the findings from the appreciative interviews were presented separately from the findings of the more conventional data collection methods. We choose to do this in order to tell the whole story that unfolded through the Appreciative Inquiry process, which could not have been fully understood if divided up and presented under each evaluation question. But to demonstrate how the use of Appreciative Inquiry methods enhanced the findings from the conventional evaluation methods, here we integrate and present both sets of findings by the three major evaluation questions.

Relationship Building with Caring Adults and Peers. In answering the evaluation question about whether the program provided opportunities for relationship building, some of the conventional methods of data collection, such as the record review, surveys, and structured observation, found that the number of activities offered and the amount of time that leaders were available to girls were key strengths in the program's delivery of service. These methods also found that there were ample opportunities for one-on-one interaction between leaders and girls and that girls received guidance and practical support from the adults over the course of the year. Both mothers and daughters reported that they could talk together about feelings, personal issues, and problems. In addition, both mothers and daughters reported that they had opportunities to resolve issues related to the mothers' incarceration. The leaders' observations gave less indication of this, and they reported being unconvinced that incarceration issues were addressed adequately.

Other conventional methods found that girls received emotional support because of the program, but more from adults than from their peers. Fewer than a third of the girls reported feeling comfortable talking with other girls in the troop; the leaders' observations were also that the peer support was poor.

The appreciative focus group interviews obtained findings somewhat different from these reports. When the girls were asked to "tell a story or give an example that shows what's best about this Girl Scout troop," many of the stories they told reflected relationship building among peers instead of relationship building with adults—for example:

"Once upon a time there was a girl named M and she got to be friends with C."
"We help each other. Like I helped my sister decorate her cake 'cause she couldn't open the icing."

One of the girls also noted, *"The best is seeing my mom."* This comment elicited vigorous head nods among others in the focus group.

Nearly all the responses from the appreciative interview and e-mail questionnaire with the Girl Scout leaders identified that the best part of the program relates to relationship building, but with both adults and peers. In regard to building relationships with adults, Girl Scout leaders had these comments:

"I see over and over how GSBB lets girls and moms talk together about their lives more, and more in-depth. It builds stronger bonds between mothers and daughters. Because of the consistency of the program, this gives the mothers more of a parenting role in their child's life. Without the program, I do not see that being possible."

"I think of some of the girls whose mothers may never be a support to them. GSBB helps girls understand, `That's my mother and I can love her, but she may not ever be there for me. It's okay that mom isn't going to be able to help me, I don't have to stop loving her. There are others who can help and support me.'"

Other Girl Scout leaders found that the best part of the program was the relationship building between the participants or peers—for example:

"I was picking up N and S (who is younger). N was GREAT with S—she mothered her, took her in hand. Took care of her. It's the bonding among girls that is best about GSBB. They have things in common. They don't have to be guarded. They can talk openly about their situations."

"S and A are two girls I've watched. They get along great despite the several year difference in age. S didn't make A feel out of place, even though she was younger. They are more helpful to each other than is true in other middle school troops I work with. They take care of each other. They're sensitive to each other's needs and are nonjudgmental. They have a connection based on, 'If you haven't experienced it, you don't know what it's all about.'"

Meaningful Involvement and Membership. The record review revealed that the number of meetings that took place during the year and the types of activities included in the meetings demonstrated that GSBB provided girls with numerous opportunities for meaningful involvement and membership. The variety of opportunities and experiences, particularly through the field trips, was quite broad. The activities offered exposure to different places and people than the girls would likely find through their schools or their family situations, such as cultural festivals and live performances, college and business tours, and camping and physical activities. Community service opportunities also were woven into many of the GSBB events.

In the surveys, girls reported feeling a sense of belonging in the Girl Scout troop, recognizing GSBB as a special program for girls like them.

Leaders observed the girls exhibiting enthusiasm for the Girl Scout traditions and appearing to understand and appreciate what Girl Scouting represents. Girls also reported feeling strongly that they were able to help others by being involved in Girl Scouts. However, the record review showed that girls did not have many opportunities to make substantial program decisions, and the survey data showed that fewer than half felt empowered to do so.

The results from the appreciative focus group interview substantiated some of these findings. They also provided additional information from the girls' perspectives about what Girl Scouting means and their feelings of connection and membership within the group. Here are some of their responses to the question of what is best about the Girl Scout troop:

"Girl Scouts helps us be responsible, do what we say we will."
"Girl Scouts teaches us to respect other people, to respect each other. Like when we talk out of turn, we know that is disrespecting."
"Girl Scouts teaches us manners."
"Once upon a time there was a girl named A and she got to know other girls just like her."
"We have privileges other girls like us don't have. We get to visit our mothers. Lots of girls don't have that privilege."

Challenging Learning Opportunities. The conventional data collection methods revealed that GSBB provided opportunities for girls to try new activities they had not participated in before. They worked on creative writing; did research; learned firsthand about various cultures, languages, and history; and went camping. They participated in activities that require cooperation and teamwork, and in environments where they were expected to behave respectfully and responsibly. Girls also were helped to practice conflict resolution.

In the survey, 85 percent of the girls agreed that they had the chance to learn new skills, 82 percent agreed that they could work better and more cooperatively with other girls in the group, and 76 percent agreed that they could help others solve disagreements. Leaders' observations were less glowing but still reasonably positive.

The findings from the appreciative focus group interview further substantiated and expanded on these findings. When identifying what is best about the Girl Scout troop, nearly half cited different opportunities and challenges the program provides—for example:

"We get to do things we've never done before and there are always surprises. Like we went camping and a bat flew in our tent."
"Once upon a time there were two girls, A and J, and we got to learn new things, like decorating cakes today."
"At Girl Scouts I get to be a girl."

"My grandmother was a Girl Scout and I like it that now I'm one."
"We help other people, like when we wrote cards for those people in the nursing home."

Common Themes. As the last step of the Appreciative Inquiry Inquire phase, the girls and Girl Scout leaders identified common themes regarding what they thought was best about the program:

Girls' Themes
• Friendship and getting to know "others like me"
• Getting to see Mom
• Opportunities to learn new things, do different things, and help others
• Respect and being responsible

Leaders' Themes
• Connection and bonding
• Support
• Stability and consistency
• Enjoyment

These themes or categories align closely with, and further confirm, the long-term outcomes identified for the program and the evaluation questions.

Because of a lack of time, neither the Girl Scout leaders nor the girls conducted the Appreciative Inquiry phases of Imagine or Innovate by imagining a better program or developing provocative propositions. However, at the girls' meeting, the evaluator asked if they could identify a motto, song lyric, or advertising jingle that captured the themes they had discussed and that they wanted to take with them into the future. The meeting was disrupted at that point by the delivery of pizza. However, in response to this request, one of the younger girls took the evaluator over to the wall where the Girl Scout Law was posted and pointed out the phrase, "I will do my best."

Benefits of Using Appreciative Inquiry

There were several benefits to using Appreciative Inquiry methods in this evaluation. The most immediate was the kind of information we received. Involving stakeholders directly in the discussion about what was best about the program and what made the best possible gave us a better understanding of what was most meaningful about the program. By obtaining additional and different insights, Appreciative Inquiry methods also complemented, expanded on, and in some cases diverged from the data collected through conventional methods. In this case, appreciatively worded questions proved to be effective in soliciting useful data relevant to program quality. In addition, and as GSBB continues, the councils will now have a fuller understanding from their key stakeholders, the girls, about what works well and what is best about the program to carry into the future.

A related benefit was the way in which Appreciative Inquiry methods fit well with the evaluation's focus. Appreciative Inquiry provided a particularly appropriate means to investigate service quality and participants' experience of the program. The more personal stories and examples clarified the girls' experience and allowed them to describe it in ways that were meaningful to them. Using Appreciative Inquiry-oriented questions helped confirm that the framework designed for the evaluation was valid and appropriate. Early on we decided to focus the evaluation on assessing the quality of service delivery and the girls' experience of the program and to use these factors as proxies for higher-level outcomes. But we often wondered whether we were looking at the right things. Were we getting at what was most important? Were we focused on the outcomes and issues that would be most useful to the organization and program staff? We believe the findings generated by using Appreciative Inquiry methods validated the evaluation design and approach.

Based on our experience with the GSBB evaluation, the use of Appreciative Inquiry methods may be particularly appropriate with asset-based programs, where the principles and purpose of Appreciative Inquiry and an increasing number of youth development, family support, education, and other client-centered programs are closely aligned. In addition, Appreciative Inquiry methods should be useful for continuing programs, in order to know from stakeholders the best parts of the program to carry forward.

Appreciative Inquiry methods may be an especially good fit with participatory evaluation approaches. As explained in Chapter One, Appreciative Inquiry and participatory evaluation share many assumptions and purposes. Where Appreciative Inquiry differs is the way in which questions are asked and the deliberate focus on eliciting the best of the program from participants. By focusing on the positive, Appreciative Inquiry aims to bring about positive change in programs. Beyond obtaining useful and meaningful data from stakeholders, Appreciative Inquiry methods could further program improvement more directly by helping stakeholders themselves recognize and build on the positive aspects of a program.

Issues in Using Appreciative Inquiry in Evaluation

The Girl Scout Councils had entered into the evaluation specifically to assess the program model and its success and how to improve program delivery. Attention to problems or program weaknesses was important to them. A common concern about an evaluation that uses solely Appreciative Inquiry methods is that it would focus only on the positive and ignore problems. In this case study, this was not an issue because Appreciative Inquiry was only one of several data collection methods. However, the glass half-full philosophy of Appreciative Inquiry should not necessarily exclude the recognition of program deficits or the need for improvement. The use of both Appreciative Inquiry and conventional evaluation methods can draw attention to both the positive and negative aspects of a program.

The use of Appreciative Inquiry in this evaluation also brought up the question of divergent findings, often evident in mixed-method approaches. The more traditional data collection methods had not demonstrated program success in terms of peer support among the girls. The stories and examples that surfaced from the Appreciative Inquiry questions pointed strongly to girls' relationships with one another as an important factor in the program. We had had concerns about whether the girls' survey accurately captured data on some of the indicators, including those related to girl-to-girl interactions. The results of the Appreciative Inquiry process demonstrate that it did not. So in this case, Appreciative Inquiry was helpful in providing a different means to explore a particularly important element of the program.

Our experience in the GSBB evaluation points to an important issue in the use of Appreciative Inquiry with program participants. Having staff available to help interpret stories provided by the girls was invaluable to our understanding of the stories' significance. For example, the girl who said that she "gets to be a girl" lives with her father and three brothers and apparently relishes the time she spends in GSBB. And the girl who talked about her grandmother being a Girl Scout will continue to live with her grandmother since her mother is incarcerated for life. The GSBB staff shared how important it was to hear the girl talk about the connection with her grandmother because the news of the mother's life sentence had been very painful and the transition to the grandmother's home had not been an easy one. This background information provided an important context for the evaluators and underscored the value of the Appreciative Inquiry process. Without the information from the staff, the stories would not have appeared particularly noteworthy.

This evaluation showed to us that using just the Inquire phase of Appreciative Inquiry could result in obtaining valuable information. In addition, the girls and Girl Scout leaders who participated in the Appreciative Inquiry process were enthusiastic in their discussions of what was best about the program. The stories shared seemed especially touching to the Girl Scout staff, eliciting deeper discussion about the meaningfulness of the program. For these reasons, the use of Appreciative Inquiry seems an important addition to our evaluation toolkit.

Areas for Further Study

Further research on Appreciative Inquiry might focus on examination of the settings, the fields, or the types of evaluation where it may not be useful or would not work well. Bushe (1998) talks about systems with "deeply held and unexpressed resentments that will not tolerate an appreciative inquiry until there has been some expression and forgiving of those resentments" (p. 1). It seems likely that stakeholders for programs with significant deficits would take a cynical view of an evaluation focused on Appreciative Inquiry. Future research might focus on circumstances that might preclude or limit the use of Appreciative Inquiry methods, where it would be inappropriate, and whether there is a wrong time to use it.

The question of using Appreciative Inquiry in evaluation as a sole data collection method versus one of several different methods also seems worth exploring. Are differences evident in the findings when looking at the two approaches? How do clients feel about the process and its results? Do they have any concerns about reporting results to their stakeholders, particularly their funders, if Appreciative Inquiry is the only data collection method used?

Further discussion of the differences in using Appreciative Inquiry for organizational development versus evaluation purposes also seems worthwhile. How are they different in approach? How are they different in outcome? Exploration of these questions would further guide evaluators interested in incorporating Appreciative Inquiry into their practice.

References

Bushe, G. R. "Five Theories of Change Embedded in Appreciative Inquiry." Paper presented at the Eighteenth Annual World Congress of Organization Development, Dublin, Ireland, July 14–18, 1998. [http://www.gervasebushe.ca/ai5.htm].

Connell, J., Gambone, M. A., and Smith, T. J. "Youth Development in Community Settings, Challenges to Our Field and Our Approach." *Youth Issues: Challenges and Directions,* Fall 2000, 281–300. [http://www.ppv.org/content/reports/ydv_pdf.html].

Gabel, K., and Johnston, D. *Children of Incarcerated Parents.* San Francisco: Jossey-Bass, 1995.

Girl Scouts Beyond Bars. Program materials. 1999.

Leffert, N., Saito, R. N., Blyth, D. A., and Kroenke, C. H. *Making the Case: Measuring the Impact of Youth Development Programs.* Minneapolis, Minn.: Search Institute, 1996.

Scales, P. C., and Leffert, N. *Developmental Assets: A Synthesis of the Scientific Research on Adolescent Development.* Minneapolis, Minn.: Search Institute, 1999.

DAWN HANSON SMART *is senior associate at Clegg & Associates in Seattle, Washington.*

MARIANN MANN *is research associate and business manager at Clegg & Associates in Seattle, Washington.*

6

This chapter argues that Appreciative Inquiry has potential in some circumstances if evaluators can successfully implement the difficult group processes and sustained engagement that it requires.

Appreciating Appreciative Inquiry

Patricia J. Rogers, Dugan Fraser

Appreciation is not just looking at the good stuff. In this chapter, we set out to appreciate Appreciative Inquiry—to develop a rounded understanding of its strengths and limitations from different perspectives and to increase its value for evaluators.

Appreciative Inquiry offers considerable promise as an addition to the evaluator's repertoire, particularly for those of us who work with a range of programs and organizations with an eye on the ultimate impact of our work, but the descriptions of Appreciative Inquiry in this volume tell only part of the story. Appreciative Inquiry can be a useful and valuable technique in the right circumstances and when well implemented, but it is not always appropriate and it requires special skills and abilities to be done properly. Nor is it only about finding nice things to say about a program.

Even for those who are not interested in adopting Appreciative Inquiry, there is much to be learned from this issue about what is needed for evaluation to effectively incorporate techniques and approaches from other disciplines and professions. Overenthusiastic promotion of any new approach to evaluation risks oversimplifying the processes involved and the demands it makes on those who seek to use it.

Thanks to John Newton, Mike Faris, Helen Goodman, and Bob Williams for their constructive, collegial discussions of Appreciative Inquiry and how it might be effectively used in evaluation.

Evaluating Approaches to Program Evaluation

Our first task is to identify desiderata for evaluating an approach to program evaluation and to be clear about our expectations for evaluation approaches. Unlike Stufflebeam (2001), we do not expect any single evaluation approach or model to be sufficient for a given evaluation and do not evaluate them in terms of their comprehensiveness. We see different evaluation approaches as components in our repertoire that can be combined as needed, not as mutually exclusive commercial products that should be adopted or rejected in their entirety. Nor do we expect any approach to be suitable for all programs, all evaluation purposes, all countries, and all organizations.

We have developed three criteria for evaluating approaches to program evaluation (Rogers, 1995). The first is the plausibility of its theory of intended impact. Program evaluation is intended to contribute to improved programs in some way (whether through formative improvement or through summative selection). What is the process by which this is expected to happen (for example, better-informed decision making, more motivated staff, engaged power brokers), and how plausible is this? The second criterion is practicality: this considers whether the technique can be successfully implemented and offers sufficient guidance for evaluation practice. The third criterion is the extent to which there is evidence that the approach works, meaning that it contributes to improved programs. On all three criteria, Appreciative Inquiry has a mixed score.

Plausibility of Its Theory of Action

Appreciative Inquiry is based on a seductively plausible causal model: that by highlighting the positive, we can help bring about the positive outcomes we describe. This is a popular and largely credible theory and the basis of many self-help books, starting with *The Power of Positive Thinking* (Peale, 1952). More recently this approach has been applied to individuals, families, organizations, and even entire countries. For example, Lundy and Visser (2003) urged South Africans to take a positive attitude to their country, arguing that attitudes shape perceptions, which shape reality. The influence of attitudes on perceptions and of perceptions on performance has been widely recognized even among nonconstructivist researchers. For example, in the Rosenthal effect (Rosenthal and Jacobsen, 1968), students randomly identified to their teachers as talented went on to improve their actual performance, despite concerns about the original study (Wineburg, 1987)—an effect of importance in learning (Murphy, Campbell, and Garavan, 1999). This appealing theory is not, however, universally appropriate or useful.

For some people, a more effective strategy is defensive pessimism, where they imagine the worst possible outcome and plan how they would cope with it (Norem, 2001). While this may seem a depressing approach, when people who use this strategy are prevented from doing so and urged to focus only on the best-case scenario, their anxiety escalates and their performance deteriorates.

In other circumstances, there is a risk that Appreciative Inquiry may encourage unrealistic and dysfunctional perceptions, attitudes, and behavior. It risks encouraging unjustified and intemperate optimism, which Lovallo and Kahneman (2003) have pointed out has undermined the quality of many executives' decisions, to the detriment of their companies. It also risks encouraging avoidance of known problems, which is rarely an effective response.

Appreciative Inquiry is based on the heliotropic principle: that people and organizations move toward those things that give them energy and life. Just as plants can grow lopsided as they reach for the light, there is a risk of distortion in what Appreciative Inquiry evaluations focus on and the activities they encourage. By seeking as explicitly for positive features as Appreciative Inquiry does, it runs the very real risk of papering over substantive problems and in fact colluding with the powerful people who want the unexamined to remain so. The original sources on Appreciative Inquiry are more thoughtful in this regard. When Cooperrider and Whitney (2000) outlined the Poetic Principle, they did not suggest that people are entirely free in the topics they choose to investigate in organizations, but acknowledged that "the topics are themselves social artifacts, products of social processes (cultural habits, typifying discourses, rhetoric, professional ways, power relations)" (p. 16). We believe that the chapters in this volume have not adequately addressed this serious issue. There is some suggestion in the cases presented here that Appreciative Inquiry can help people in organizations to face up to previously identified problems, but the evidence is sparse.

We are also concerned about the overemphasis on how perceptions affect reality without due concern for how reality can intrude on people's lives. There are many aspects of lived reality that are not invented and exist despite our mental state; grinding poverty, gender inequality, violence, and disease are some examples.

Given these limitations on the universality of Appreciative Inquiry, in which contexts is Appreciative Inquiry's theory of action most likely to be appropriate and effective? It seems that Appreciative Inquiry is likely to be most useful when the purpose of the evaluation is not to identify unknown problems but to identify strengths (both those that are known and unknown) and build courage to attend to known problems.

Appreciative Inquiry can help to identify and make explicit areas of good performance and to communicate and institutionalize what is already known about good performance so that it gets continued or replicated. Appreciative Inquiry seems less likely to be useful when bad performance is not yet known and needs to be discovered. It is important to note that in all the cases in these chapters, previous evaluation work had identified problems. This suggests that Appreciative Inquiry might be a useful complement to deficit-focused evaluations, which can leave organizations frayed and distressed. In such a context, Appreciative Inquiry may be a useful strategy to remind stakeholders of the value the initiative offers and to suggest ways of capitalizing and building on what is good. It may also be particularly useful and invigorating for staff whose day-to-day work has become disconnected from their ultimate goals and who can use the resulting information to revise planned activities, objectives, and targets and reconnect them with their deep aspirations. Instead of seeing program evaluation as a process of generating and communicating new knowledge, Appreciative Inquiry suggests that it might be fundamentally a process of "locating the energy for change," as one Appreciative Inquiry publication is titled (Elliott, 1999).

Guidance for Practice

It is difficult to provide sufficient guidance for practice when introducing a new approach that is based on substantial literature and requires high-level skills. Nevertheless, we are concerned about the quality of guidance that is provided for evaluators in this collection. The version of Appreciative Inquiry that is described here treats appreciation as involving an exclusive focus on the positive, which does not do justice to the complexity of Appreciative Inquiry. That important features of Appreciative Inquiry and the difficulties in successfully implementing the approach are not adequately described worries us. Evaluators may underestimate the skills needed to implement this approach effectively and thus not be prepared for dealing with potential problems should they arise. It may be that evaluators need to team with experienced and skilled organizational development facilitators to implement this approach effectively.

We would urge readers who are interested in Appreciative Inquiry to read more broadly, in particular Elliott's account (1999) of using Appreciative Inquiry in a project working with street children in Africa. Elliott makes it clear that Appreciative Inquiry involves developing a deeper understanding of the program, which requires prolonged engagement, a commitment to empirical investigation, and progressive investigation of different perspectives. His frank discussion of the difficulties they faced provides useful guidance to evaluators attempting to use the technique.

Elliott also argues that the appreciative approach should be collaborative across as broad a spectrum of stakeholders as possible rather than be confined to one dominant group. It should issue provocative or challenging propositions that stretch the mind of everyone in the organization to new vistas of the possible rather than being a rehash of groupthink.

Evaluators need more guidance on how to effectively engage a broad spectrum of stakeholders, including addressing the power issues that will necessarily be involved. One of our main concerns around Appreciative

Inquiry is its potential to involve and include program staff (who are better able to participate in more of the processes) at the expense of program beneficiaries, and in this way to deepen and widen the gap between those who are already empowered and those who are not. Smart and Mann (Chapter Five, this volume) described their difficulties in successfully engaging program beneficiaries in an Appreciative Inquiry exercise.

Evidence That It Works

In addition to the evidence from the cases and other published accounts of Appreciative Inquiry, we have had personal experience of the positive energy generated by Appreciative Inquiry. A presentation on Appreciative Inquiry by Hallie Preskill at the Evaluator's Institute in Washington, D.C., in 2001 generated tremendous excitement and enthusiasm. The questions were about peak experiences doing evaluation, and the buzz across the room as we discussed these in pairs was electrifying. The experience of that energy and enthusiasm was very powerful. The challenge, however, is not in generating the energy but in sustaining it and directing it in useful ways. Appreciative Inquiry is not a brief exercise with program staff but a sustained and difficult process, involving diverse stakeholders and empirical investigation of the program.

The cases in this volume provide varied evidence of the feasibility and utility of Appreciative Inquiry. McNamee's account in Chapter Two of an Appreciative Inquiry intervention in a private high school in the United States details a very developed version of Appreciative Inquiry. The case described sustained engagement and genuine efforts to understand different perspectives and share these with the affected group, as well as a commitment to following through with subsequent planning and implementation of changes. What emerges clearly from the account is that care, extensive preparation, and great sensitivity are needed to make the technique successful. We were particularly impressed with the way the critical comments of staff were gathered at the beginning of the process and included later in the process, while maintaining confidentiality and the focus on the positive. It is important to note, however, that two important groups of stakeholders—students and their parents—were not apparently included in the process.

Catsambas and Webb's case study in Chapter Three of their work with the International Women's Media Foundation documents the care they took to follow the right procedures, including important components such as careful regular reporting back and postevaluation follow-ups. This case shows very clearly that Appreciative Inquiry is not an easy way to make people feel uncritically good about their programs but is instead a challenging and demanding approach to program evaluation. There are clearly limits, however, to the extent to which evaluators are willing to frankly discuss difficulties and limitations in their work, and any account that depends on only retrospective accounts by evaluators risks accusations of being self-serving.

Jacobsgaard's case study in Chapter Four of the Family Rehabilitation Centre in Sri Lanka is one in which the appreciative process was left unfinished, though the exercise appears nevertheless to have had a positive impact. In this case, elements of Appreciative Inquiry were used with other methods to support and promote healing in an organization previously bruised by insensitive and damaging evaluations that had undermined participants and staff (it is interesting how often an evaluation parallels the type of program the organization runs). Appreciative Inquiry returns here to its roots in organizational development, where it clearly has enormous positive potential. This case suggests that the process of Appreciative Inquiry helped people in the organization to address known problems. However, more information and more discussion of the subsequent activities would have added to the weight of evidence that this case provides.

We were less convinced that Smart and Mann's case in Chapter Five on Girl Scouts Beyond Bars provides evidence of the implementation or impact of Appreciative Inquiry. The program being evaluated was clearly a valuable one, but the study reduced Appreciative Inquiry to a simple matter of including some open-ended questions in an interview schedule, neither discussing how this fell short of comprehensive Appreciative Inquiry nor explaining why this was done. We do not advocate purism, but to categorize a study as an exercise in Appreciative Inquiry requires more than the use of a few basic procedures.

Using Appreciative Inquiry for Evaluation

The cases in this collection suggest that Appreciative Inquiry is likely to be at its most useful in long-standing programs that have become depleted or exhausted and require an infusion of positive energy and recognition in order to be revived and that have also completed more usual evaluations that have identified the problems that exist. Appreciative Inquiry is particularly valuable in programs that are highly complex, where the technique can serve to restate and reframe what is valuable, useful, and important.

Appreciative Inquiry is a good choice if the necessary skills and capacities are in place to manage and guide the process. When multidisciplinary teams are being assembled, consideration should be given to including members who have the affirming types of skills needed to apply the technique properly and to include elements of the approach in their evaluation strategies. Without the necessary facilitation and group work skills, we suspect that Appreciative Inquiry could go dangerously wrong, leading to vacuous, self-congratulatory findings (by avoiding hard issues and uncomplimentary data); even worse, Appreciative Inquiry could provide a platform for airing vengeful and destructive sentiments by drawing implicit comparisons between ideal performance and the performance of those present.

More General Lessons for Evaluation Practice

These accounts of Appreciative Inquiry offer important lessons for evaluation practice, even for those who do not adopt it. One of its major strengths is its fundamental recognition that an evaluation is an intervention that causes ripples in the life of an institution. Many evaluators operate without recognition of this fact, and they proceed with their assessments in ways that are insensitive to the impact their questions and investigations have on the life of an organization or institution. Anxiety, tension, and even serious forms of dishonesty can be triggered by insensitive evaluations and can have long-term effects on initiatives, directly and indirectly. It is important that the impact that evaluations have on organizations be considered and factored in when selecting techniques to be used to gather, analyze, report, and use information.

More generally, these accounts raise issues about the way in which we should develop, implement, document, and report new approaches to evaluation. One of these issues is how comprehensive and faithful to key principles a case needs to be in order to be considered an example of that approach.

Bushe (2000) makes the important point that as Appreciative Inquiry becomes fashionable, "any inquiry that focuses on the positive in some way gets called appreciative inquiry. . . . The result will be that the unique power of this idea gets corrupted and lost and Appreciative Inquiry becomes just another discarded innovation on the junk heap of 'failed' management effectiveness strategies" (p. 99).

Implementation fidelity is an important issue in any evaluation that seeks to generalize about an approach. It is made more difficult when evaluating evaluations, which might quite reasonably combine elements of different approaches or adapt to local conditions. We need to decide what elements of an approach need to be in place for it to be considered an example of its use.

The cases also raise issues about presenting new approaches and accounts of evaluation practice. Ideally, discussions of new approaches should not present a straw man of other approaches or oversimplify the new approach. Ideally accounts of evaluation practice should provide more evidence of sustained benefits and corroboration from people other than the evaluators.

We do not need more narratives of the evaluator as hero, and we do not need evaluation models to be marketed as if they were competing commercial products. Rather, we need better documentation of accounts of evaluation practice, and we need to see evaluation models as being based on and using complementary skills and ideas.

Conclusion

This volume is a valuable and constructive contribution to program evaluation because it offers examples of good practice as well as how Appreciative Inquiry can fall short. Noting these lessons and learning from the experiences of others puts us in a better position to improve our own practice and to contribute to performance improvement in meaningful ways.

References

Bushe, G. R. "Five Theories of Change Embedded in Appreciative Inquiry." In D. L. Cooperrider, P. Sorenson, D. Whitney, and T. Yeager (eds.), *Appreciative Inquiry: An Emerging Direction for Organization Development.* Champaign, Ill.: Stipes, 2000.

Cooperrider, D. L., and Whitney, D. "A Positive Revolution in Change: Appreciative Inquiry." In D. Cooperrider, P. F. Sorensen, D. Whitney, and T. F. Yaeger (eds.), *Appreciative Inquiry: Rethinking Human Organization Toward a Positive Theory of Change.* Champaign, Ill.: Stipes Publishing, 2000.

Elliott, C. *Locating the Energy for Change: An Introduction to Appreciative Inquiry.* Winnipeg, Manitoba: International Institute for Sustainable Development, 1999. [http://iisd1.iisd.ca/pdf/appreciativeinquiry.pdf].

Lovallo, D., and Kahneman, D. "Deluded by Success: How Optimism Undermines Executives' Decisions." *Harvard Business Review,* 2003, *51*(6), 56–63.

Lundy, G., and Visser, W. *South Africa: Reasons to Believe.* Cape Town, South Africa: Aardvark Press, 2003.

Murphy, D., Campbell, C., and Garavan, T. "The Pygmalion Effect Reconsidered: Its Implications for Education, Training, and Workplace Learning." *Journal of European Industrial Training,* 1999, *23*(4/5), 238–251.

Norem, J. *The Positive Power of Negative Thinking: Using Defensive Pessimism to Harness Anxiety and Perform at Your Peak.* New York: Basic Books, 2001.

Peale, N. V. *The Power of Positive Thinking.* Englewood Cliffs, N.J.: Prentice Hall, 1952.

Rogers, P. J. "Evaluating Evaluation by Analysing Its Impact on Programs." Proceedings of the International Conference of the Australasian Evaluation Society. Sydney, Australia, 1995.

Rosenthal, R. "Pygmalion Effects: Existence, Magnitude and Social Importance: A Reply to Wineburg." *Educational Researcher,* 1987, *16*(9), 37–40.

Rosenthal, R., and Jacobsen, L. *Pygmalion in the Classroom: Teacher Expectation and Pupils' Intellectual Development.* Austin, Tex.: Holt, Rinehart and Winston, 1968.

Stufflebeam, D. L. (ed.). *Evaluation Models.* New Directions for Evaluation, no. 89. San Francisco: Jossey-Bass, 2001.

Wineburg, S. S. "The Self-Fulfillment of the Self-Fulfilling Prophecy: A Critical Appraisal." *Educational Researcher,* 1987, *16*(9), 28–37.

PATRICIA J. ROGERS is associate professor in public sector evaluation at the Collaborative Institute for Research, Consulting and Learning in Evaluation, Royal Melbourne Institute of Technology, Australia.

DUGAN FRASER is a consultant in monitoring and evaluation with southern African nongovernmental organizations and the South African Public Service Commission.

7

Appreciative Inquiry evaluation offers an important new option in evaluation's increasingly vast repertoire of approaches. Its ultimate legitimacy and credibility will depend on how it is applied and used.

Inquiry into Appreciative Evaluation*

Michael Quinn Patton

> Words are loaded pistols.
>
> —Jean Paul Sartre

I had occasion to open another *New Directions for Evaluation* chapter with this Sartre quotation (Patton, 2000), in a volume titled *How and Why Language Matters in Evaluation* (Hopson, 2000). The contributors to this current volume make the case that the language of appreciation matters; it matters in general and it matters in evaluation. The controversy engendered by this notion suggests that the word *appreciation* is one of the bullets in Sartre's pistol, at least when used in a supposedly evaluative context. Indeed, the case examples shared in this volume demonstrate that the pistol is not just loaded but has already been fired.

The peaceful idea of appreciation clashes with the violent metaphor of a loaded pistol, but this juxtaposition is purposeful, perhaps even instructive. Many with whom I have talked insist that a preordinate mind-set of appreciation does violence to the very idea of evaluation. They find appreciation as a way of framing evaluation by turns anathema, oxymoronic, cacophonous, and even dangerous. So, I open with violence. Later, I'll work in a little sex. With that we will have covered the two pillars of contemporary American society. First, I propose a little walk down the memory lane of organizational development.

_____

*A Staggering and Heartbreaking Examination of Appreciative Evaluation Complete with Controversy, Violence and Sex, Not to Mention Ramblings, Conjectures, Opinions, Judgments, and Appreciations, This Being a Brazen Allusion to a Best-Selling Gen-X Book (Eggers, 2000) in the Faint Hope That My Antiquity Would Be Disguised and That This Would Attract Gen-Xers to Evaluation, Thereby Serving to Propagate the Profession and Fulfill the Promise of Sex if Not of Violence.

New Directions for Evaluation, no. 100, Winter 2003   © Wiley Periodicals, Inc.

Appreciative Inquiry as Organizational Development

Proposals for *New Directions for Evaluation* undergo rigorous peer review. In reviewing proposals for this volume, the peer reviewers were particularly insistent that the case examples be genuinely evaluative in nature, not just examples of organizational development (OD). This feedback is sensible given the mission of the journal, and it seems to me that the contributors have followed this mandate and provided real evaluation applications of Appreciative Inquiry. But while sensible and understandable, I want to suggest that the distinction may be overdrawn and, in certain circumstances, which I find increasing, unhelpful. Here is why. It is the classic a-rose-by-any-other-name argument. Sometimes it is helpful and appropriate to call an evaluative inquiry just that. Sometimes, because of the preconceptions and negative connotations associated with evaluation or a program's bad experiences with evaluators, either of which can be substantial barriers to openness and utility, the process may proceed more smoothly and engagingly if called organizational development (OD). This may seem like a bit of a bait-and-switch scam, but I call it doing what works, what is useful. Especially in program settings and agencies where being a learning organization is the order of the day, the supposed boundaries and distinctions between OD and evaluation can get in the way of getting on with learning and improvement whatever it is called, even "Appreciative Inquiry."

The profession of program evaluation has developed parallel to the professions of management consulting and organization development. OD consultants advise on and facilitate a variety of change processes, including solving communications problems, conflict resolution, strategic planning, leadership development, teamwork, human resource development, diversity training, shaping organizational culture, organizational learning, and defining mission, to name but a few OD arenas of action. Sometimes their methods include organizational surveys and field observations, and they may facilitate action research as a basis for problem solving. They may even do evaluations.

Evaluators also engage routinely in development work as part of comprehensive evaluations. Logic modeling is a prime example. From exchanges on EVALTALK (the American Evaluation Association Internet listserv) and presentations at national evaluation conferences throughout the world, it appears that evaluators are engaged in a great deal of logic modeling, clarifying and building program theory, or otherwise engaging in conceptual mapping exercises to help program staff and other organizational stakeholders figure out what they are doing and why they think they are doing it. This sounds very much like program design and development. But it is also a critical evaluability assessment exercise, building the foundation for subsequent meaningful evaluation.

Evaluators have been influenced by and begun drawing on OD (Patton, 1999; Preskill and Torres, 1999; Torres and Preskill, 2001). And in a spirit of mutuality, I think we can modestly say that professional evaluators have a great deal to offer OD initiatives and processes. Evaluation's niche is defined by its emphasis on reality testing, that is, helping users determine the extent to which what they think and hope is going on is what is actually going on. (I am using *reality testing* in its day-to-day, commonsense meaning and am not attempting to provoke an epistemological argument— or fire another chamber of the loaded language gun.) The processes of evaluation support change in organizations by helping those involved think empirically, whether capturing, testing, interpreting, and reporting singular or multiple realities, providing realist or constructivist feedback, using qualitative or quantitative data, or a mix. Evaluators teach the methods and utility of data-based decision making. This can include exposing stakeholders to and training them in the logic and values of evaluation in support of becoming learning organizations—an example of what I have called the process use of evaluation, that is, helping people in organizations learn to think evaluatively so as to build evaluation into the organizational culture and engage in evaluation as part of ongoing OD (Patton, 1997).

Many program and project evaluators have been unnecessarily self-limiting in the face of OD opportunities by defining the primary unit of analysis for evaluation as the program or project and thereby missing the larger, and crucial, organizational context within which the project or program operates. The open-ended nature of Appreciative Inquiry story gathering makes it possible to transcend units of analysis. When asked what they value, respondents do not have to be constrained by whether their response is within project boundaries or reflects the larger organizational culture.

The question of organizational effectiveness can feel quite different from program or project effectiveness. The evaluation challenge typically becomes more complex at the organizational level. There may be more stakeholders to deal with, more levels of stakeholders, and therefore greater challenges in sorting through various interests, interpersonal dynamics, and organizational politics. The environment surrounding and influencing an organization may also be more complex and dynamic compared to the environment of a single program. Operating at the organizational level may also increase the possibility of having impact by being able to deal directly with those who have the power to make changes.

From a systems perspective, because programs and projects are usually embedded in larger organizational contexts, improving programs and projects may be linked to and even dependent on changing the organizations of which they are a part. John Brandl, former director of the Humphrey Institute of Public Affairs at the University of Minnesota, as well as a former state legislator, made this point in a 1988 keynote address to the American Evaluation Association in New Orleans. Focusing especially on the effectiveness of government-supported programs, he argued that evaluators needed to examine, understand, and assess the ways in which being part of larger bureaucracies affects program and project effectiveness. He went on

to suggest that factors affecting staff motivation, efficiency of program processes, and incentives to achieve outcomes would be found at the organizational level more than at the program or project level. Thus, improving
programs necessarily means developing greater organizational effectiveness.

Appreciative Inquiry as Another Evaluation Option

I have begun by questioning the rigid distinction between OD and evaluation because it seems to me that Appreciative Inquiry is best understood and
appreciated as first and foremost an approach to organizational and program
development. Adapted to evaluation, to evaluative opportunities and challenges, it offers another option for undertaking learning-and-development-
oriented evaluation, adding to the increasingly rich array of developmental
diversity within evaluation that includes participatory evaluation, collaborative evaluation, empowerment evaluation, inclusive evaluation, developmental evaluation, multivocal evaluation, learning-oriented evaluation,
democratic evaluation, feminist evaluation, and now Appreciative Inquiry
evaluation, or simply appreciative evaluation.

Chapter One provided an in-depth review of Appreciative Inquiry's
development. Conceived and described in the work of David Cooperrider
and his colleagues at Case Western Reserve's school of organization behavior (Watkins and Cooperrider, 2000), Appreciative Inquiry is being offered
by its advocates as "a worldview, a paradigm of thought and understanding
that holds organizations to be affirmative systems created by humankind as
solutions to problems. It is a theory, a mindset, and an approach to analysis that leads to organizational learning and creativity" (p. 6). As such,
"[Appreciative Inquiry] reflects the core values of OD," stated editors
Sorensen, Yaeger, and Nicoll (2000, p. 4) in introducing a special issue of
the journal *OD Practitioner* devoted to Appreciative Inquiry.

Appreciative Inquiry integrates inquiry and action within a particular
developmental framework that guides analysis and processes of group interaction. The qualitative questioning and thematic analysis processes constitute a form of intervention by the very nature of the questions asked and the
assets-oriented framework used to guide analysis. In this way, inquiry and
action are completely integrated. Other forms of participatory inquiry also
seek integration of inquiry and action. Appreciative Inquiry adds a distinctly
different and highly systematic way of conducting evaluations. Or does it? Is
it really evaluative? Or is it *only* developmental and, as such, should be left
within OD without contaminating evaluation? Evaluation theorists are
divided on this issue.

Defining Evaluation

Such are the dilemmas and consternations of the profession's openness
and diversity, which invite different perspectives to debate and compete and
requires each evaluator to determine his or her own definitional preference.

I feel no need for a definitive, authority-based definition, and I do not expect one to emerge despite the lamentations of those unsettled and confused by our diversity. It just means that we each bear the responsibility to be clear about what we mean by evaluation. The importance of this commentary to the matter at hand is that how one defines evaluation will determine to a great extent whether Appreciative Inquiry is considered an evaluation option.

I made a similar observation in a *New Directions for Evaluation* volume devoted to feminist evaluation in a chapter entitled, "Feminist, Yes, But Is It Evaluation?" (Patton, 2002). It turns out that the various definitions of evaluation do not just tell you what you must do; they can be interpreted, and often are, as saying that is *all* you can do. If evaluation is defined as judgment of merit and worth—do that and do only that. Everything else must be something other than evaluation. If evaluation is defined as the application of social science methods to determine program effectiveness, do that and only that. Anything else is of lesser value or even illegitimate. If evaluation is defined as determining the extent to which a program achieves its goals, that becomes the priority task, and all else is at best secondary, if even worth the bother.

The objections to Appreciative Inquiry evaluation do not center on the inquiry part of the terminological equation. The objections flow from concern with the oxymoronic nature of the combination of the terms *appreciative* and *evaluation*. Let us take this definitional challenge at face value. The question of what constitutes evaluation requires criteria, as does the even more devilish question of what constitutes "good" or high-quality evaluation. Credibility flows from those judgments. Quality and credibility are connected in that judgments of quality constitute the foundation for perceptions of credibility. Appreciative Inquiry evaluation appears to challenge, even undermine, such traditional criteria for assessing evaluations as balance, independence, neutrality, and minimal bias.

In contrast, pragmatic and utilitarian criteria emphasize the importance of a match between the values and perspectives of primary intended users of an evaluation and the evaluator. Thus, by those criteria, the question becomes what kinds of evaluation opportunities are especially appropriate for Appreciative Inquiry evaluation. Utilization-focused evaluation practitioners, for example, present primary intended users with a range of options, facilitate their understanding of the strengths and weaknesses of those options, and then help them determine the best fit for those needs. In that process, Appreciative Inquiry evaluation can be a viable and important option in utilization-focused evaluations, especially where evaluation and developmental purposes overlap and are mutually reinforcing. Pragmatic and utilitarian criteria do not inherently conflict with Appreciative Inquiry evaluation principles as long as primary intended users choose Appreciative Inquiry evaluation because they see it as particularly appropriate for their situation.

This means that understanding the situations that are good candidates for Appreciative Inquiry is critical. Chapter One provides a helpful list in this regard, worth reproducing here:

• Where previous evaluation efforts have failed
• Where there is a fear of or skepticism about evaluation
• With varied groups of stakeholders who know little about each other or the program being evaluated
• Within hostile or volatile environments
• When change needs to be accelerated
• When dialogue is critical to moving the organization forward
• When relationships among individuals and groups have deteriorated and there is a sense of hopelessness
• When there is a desire to build evaluation capacity—to help others learn from evaluation practice
• When there is a desire to build a community of practice
• When it is important to increase support for evaluation and possibly the program being evaluated

The case examples reported in this volume affirm and add to this list and illustrate and reinforce the importance of matching the evaluation approach to the specific situation encountered. Sheila McNamee reports in Chapter Two how appreciative inquiry worked within a "conflicted educational context." She provides detailed description of her approach to the process, how she worked along the way, what she said, and how people responded. The process was designed and facilitated to bring about change, not just yield data. In addition, and as this case suggests, evaluation from an appreciative stance can facilitate collaboration among participants.

The context for Mette Jacobsgaard's example from Sri Lanka in Chapter Four is a program that had recently received a negative progress evaluation. The evaluators struggled with meeting the mandate to report on outcomes while staying true to the appreciative format. Taking an Appreciative Inquiry approach "defused a possible tension among the FRC staff who expected the evaluation to focus on where they had failed, as they had experienced in previous evaluations. Thus, by focusing on what had worked well and why it had worked, the staff were more willing to tell their stories." The overall impact, as reported, appears to have been quite high:

> As I have reflected on this evaluation, I am convinced that the information gathered had very different qualities and was much richer than it would have been had we used a more traditional problem-focused approach to the evaluation and the interview questions. By grounding the wishes and dreams for the future in the staff's stories, they came to own the resulting recommendations that came out of the provocative propositions. I also believe that in the end, the FRC staff had more positive energy to carry their work forward. Building on the knowledge of where and how FRC had succeeded gave them the motivation and creativity to solve the problems that often seemed insurmountable. In fact, one of FRC's senior managers proceeded to take an

Appreciative Inquiry training course following the evaluation and has now introduced Appreciative Inquiry as the operational approach in FRC.

In Chapter Five, Dawn Hanson Smart and Mariann Mann reported using selected aspects of Appreciative Inquiry in the third year of an evaluation of Girl Scouts Beyond Bars, a scouting program for girls whose mothers are incarcerated. They reported that one reason for choosing Appreciative Inquiry was because of its fit with the asset-based scouting program. Assets analysis (Patton, 1987) is not the opposite of needs assessment. Rather, it highlights a different aspect of the assessment process. Where needs assessment suggests deficiencies to be corrected, assets analysis calls attention to strengths that can be developed. Just as programs are often unaware of the needs of their clients, so too they are often unaware of the capabilities of their clients. Those strengths or assets, if known, can be used to help clients meet their own needs. Thus, we have witnessed great interest in identifying community assets (Kretzmann and McKnight, 1997; Mattessich and Monsey, 1997), organizational assets, and youth assets (Leffert and others, 1998). Assets analysis provides a counterbalance to needs assessment. Both phrases are examples of how the language we use directs our attention toward some things and away from others, a common theme of this volume. As Smart and Mann illustrate, Appreciative Inquiry is especially appropriate for and congruent with programs based on an assets model.

Tessie Tzavaras Catsambas and Laverne Webb present in Chapter Three a midterm evaluation of an international nonprofit's African center. Appreciative Inquiry seemed well suited for this evaluation because the client required a combination of credibility, sensitivity, and honesty and data that would be useful in designing the future of the program. This case calls our attention to Appreciative Inquiry's value where those in the program are as interested in looking to the future as they are assessing the past.

The Issue of Balance

Still, despite these examples and apparent successes in applying Appreciative Inquiry for evaluative purposes, the notion of an appreciative framework for evaluation will rankle some. Appreciative Inquiry has been criticized for being unbalanced and uncritical in its emphasis (critics say overemphasis) on accentuating the positive. It may even, ironically, discourage inquiry by discouraging constructive criticism (Golembiewski, 2000). The focus on appreciation can imply an unwillingness to look at weaknesses, problems, and things that are going wrong. Yet the cases in this volume provide strong evidence that problems and weaknesses can and do emerge in an appreciation-centered inquiry. Moreover, the cases even provide evidence that some problems and weaknesses can be easier to address and surface when evaluation takes an appreciative stance; that was the experience of Jacobsgaard in Sri Lanka.

I can provide some additional evidence on this point. Shortly after agreeing to participate in this volume, I had the opportunity to facilitate part of an Appreciative Inquiry process. A Unitarian congregation with a new pastoral team wanted to evaluate the effectiveness of church programs as a basis for future planning and resource allocation. A congregational member suggested Appreciative Inquiry and directed the data-gathering process as part of her master's degree work, adhering rigorously to the 4-D process described in Chapter One. Because she lacked experience facilitating qualitative analysis, I was sought out to take the board and pastoral team through the analytical process. It was clear from the outset that the Appreciative Inquiry framework was congruent with the congregation's values. Both politically and philosophically, the new pastoral team believed it would facilitate the leadership transition, which was traumatic for some church members, if the new team approached the exercise appreciating what had gone before and making past strengths the foundation for future changes. In short, there appeared to be a good match between the appreciative form of inquiry, the purpose of the evaluation, and the values of those of involved. Having satisfied myself on that score, I focused on the question of evaluative balance. Did the data reveal strengths and weaknesses, and assets and problems? Did the process yield complaints as well as kudos?

As others have reported in this volume, the "dreams" or "wishes" questions provided the greatest opportunity for balance. There was no shortage of dreams that indicated existing weaknesses from the perspective of the dreamers:

"I dream about singing good-old-fashioned hymns instead of all these new songs that I don't know the words to and don't recognize the tunes of."
"My wish is that we someday have more young adults actively involved in the congregation."
"I dream of diversity, and I've been dreaming about it for years, and it doesn't look like a dream that's going to come true in my lifetime."
"I want meaningful, interesting sermons that send me home inspired. Is that too much to ask?"
"I long for a Sunday school program that my kids actually want to come to."

As you can see, and as others have indicated in their case reports in this volume, an Appreciative Inquiry process that is open, inviting, and trusted can generate plenty of data about perceived weaknesses and concerns.

Problematic Roots

Speaking of weakness, and in the interest of balance, let me raise a concern about some problematic assumptions from which Appreciative Inquiry was derived. One of the frequent responsibilities we incur as evaluators is trying to determine how much of what people in a program believe is myth and how much is in some way evidence based. This is often not an easy task, but knowing the difference can be important. The same is true in examining models.

Chapter One in this volume identified some of the early influences on Appreciative Inquiry: "The first such finding was the placebo effect, in which one- to two-thirds of patients showed marked improvement in symptoms by believing they had received effective treatment." It is perhaps worth noting that in some quarters there is considerable skepticism about the placebo effect. Jones (2003) reviewed evidence on the placebo effect and concluded that the evidence is quite flimsy, more a matter of folklore than science:

> Placebos have no effect on ailments that can be measured objectively, such as cholesterol levels and blood pressure. There is no placebo action on immune function. . . . What kinds of things have emerged as the real causes of "placebo" improvement? There are all manner of subjective ailments that vary from day-to-day, and even from minute to minute: headache, stomachache, tension. It is very difficult to come up with a meaningful measure of change in disorders like these. Pain itself is notoriously difficult to measure objectively. The American Society of Pain Management Nurses and the Oncology Nursing Society have gone on record against using placebos therapeutically. . . .
>
> There are many other known causes of apparent medical improvement: patient expectation; the desire to please the doctor; misattributing true cause-and-effect; ignorance of the random fluctuations of most disorders; regression to the mean; and the demand characteristics of the patient-doctor relationship [Jones, 2003, p. 12].

The authors of Chapter One note, "A second set of influential findings was from the Pygmalion studies, which demonstrated the relationship between the images teachers have of their students and the students' levels of performance and long-term futures." Here again some caution appears to be in order. In an article that has become a classic, Samuel Wineburg (1987) conducted a critical review of Pygmalion studies and found that the Pygmalion interpretation has assumed "mythic proportions" despite weak, inconsistent, and contradictory evidence and the "reports of Pygmalion in the press showed how the study came to stand for whatever people wanted it to, regardless of the original research" (p. 31). His critique was critiqued in turn by Pygmalion effects researcher and advocate Robert Rosenthal. Let me add, appreciatively, that the back-and-forth exchange between Wineburg and Rosenthal featured in the December 1987 issue of *Educational Researcher* is one of the finest examples I've encountered of scholarly debate and the challenges of interpreting research to inform action.

Appreciative Inquiry will and should ultimately be judged on its merits—on its utility and contributions. One need not believe in either the placebo effect or the self-fulfilling prophecy to employ Appreciative Inquiry. Nevertheless, the placebo effect and the self-fulfilling prophecy are so deeply ingrained in Western culture and so overgeneralized in their application that any model built on them invites skepticism. I would be inclined to downplay that part of Appreciative Inquiry's roots when introducing it to a new audience so as to avoid engendering a tangential debate. I would also be inclined to examine just how important these beliefs are to Appreciative Inquiry in practice.

The Shaping Power of Language: Alternative Ways of Framing Evaluative Questions

It is clear that the language of Appreciative Inquiry evaluation shapes the perspective of those involved. That is the purpose of the language. It is the purpose of any label or title. I have already contrasted needs assessment and assets analysis as offering different foci. The contrast is worth exploring further. A number of evaluators, most notably Michael Scriven, have made needs assessment the first and most fundamental step in program development and evaluation. The funding of many programs is contingent on conducting some kind of needs assessment. The concept of needs assessment focuses on and calls attention to the premise that programs first and foremost should serve client needs—not staff needs, political needs, organizational needs, or funder needs. Needs assessment is a powerful conceptual frame—perhaps too powerful say those who express concern that the focus on client needs has become so pervasive and dominant that program staff and evaluators have largely ignored client strengths and assets (thus the current popularity of assets-based programs illustrated by Smart and Mann in Chapter Five). The contrast raises this question: Is needs assessment balanced? One can make the case that needs assessment is as unbalanced as Appreciative Inquiry, only in the opposite direction. Indeed, I might speculate that an Appreciative Inquiry evaluation is more likely to turn up problems and weaknesses (unmet needs) than a needs assessment is likely to turn up assets and strengths. Of course, in both instances, it all depends on how—and how well—it is done.

Another illustration of how a shift in language can affect evaluation focus and relationships comes from the work of Sharon Rallis and Gretchen Rossman (2000). In contrast to Appreciative Inquiry, they described their evaluator role as "critical friend." Especially when the primary purpose of evaluation is learning, the role of critical friend, they argue, allows them as evaluators to engage in "dialogue" instead of relying on the traditional evaluator's "language of authority."

It is informative how slight and nuanced shifts in language can imply quite different meanings. Perhaps the most widely cited definition of and

Table 7.1. Two Sets of Evaluation Questions

Appreciative Inquiry	Inquiry into Merit and Worth
Looking at your entire experience with the organization, remember a time when you felt most alive, most fulfilled, or most excited about your involvement in the organization.	Looking at your entire experience with the program, remember a time when you felt that your work had the greatest merit or worth. Tell us about that time. What made the worth meritorious? What gave it worth?
Let's talk for a moment about some things you value deeply; specifically, the things you value about yourself, about the nature of your work, and about this organization.	Let's talk for a moment about making judgments of merit and worth, specifically, how you make judgments about the merit and worth of the things you value about what you do, about the merit and worth of your work and this program.
What do you experience as the core factors that give life to this organization? Give some examples of how you experience those factors.	What do you experience as the core results that demonstrate the merit and worth of this program? Give some examples of how you experience and recognize those results.
What three wishes would you make to heighten the vitality and health of this organization?	What three wishes would you make to increase the merit and worth of this program?

Source: For column 1: Watkins and Cooperrider (2000, p. 9).

purpose for program evaluation is the one that undergirds the Joint Committee on Standards for Educational Evaluation Program Evaluation Standards (1994): the purpose of evaluation is to judge merit and worth. The left column of Table 7.1 sets out questions offered by Watkins and Cooperrider as ideal-typical Appreciative Inquiry questions. The right column has questions for what I shall call "Merit and Worth Evaluation."

I leave to readers to consider how the insertion of different words changes and shapes the focus of the inquiry. How does the shift from appreciation to merit and worth change what is implied? Asked in these ways, what about the questions in each column make them balanced or unbalanced? To what extent are the questions in each column genuinely open? Leading? Evocative? Evaluative?

Appreciative Inquiry and Utilization-Focused Evaluation

The frame I bring to judging the merit and worth of any particular evaluation is its utility and actual use (Patton, 1997). This being no great secret and having compared Appreciative Inquiry with the hypothetical merit and worth evaluation approach, it seems only fair to examine some of the premises of utilization-focused evaluation that have corollaries in Appreciative Inquiry evaluation (see Table 7.2).

Table 7.2 contrasts Appreciative Inquiry principles set out in Chapter One with some utilization-focused evaluation premises. Although the specific language and focus vary, interesting and informative congruencies can be located—if congruence is what one seeks. Yet again, it is all a matter of perspective. I can find similarities. I can find differences. I can find similarities *and* differences. And this takes me back to the principle of situational responsiveness: matching the evaluation approach to the needs, assets, and interests of primary intended users. Appreciative Inquiry strikes me as a viable and useful option in the situations described earlier.

Evaluation Will Be Affected by Whatever Is Hot

Evaluation, not being an ivory tower activity (at least not primarily, though there are exceptions), is influenced by trends, hopes, and fads in the larger world. Whatever is hot in the corporate world quickly finds its way into the government, nonprofit, and philanthropic sectors and into evaluation. Appreciative Inquiry has become hot. It may be in part a backlash against the cynicism of our age. In that regard, I am told by a colleague of David Cooperrider (Appreciative Inquiry's founding influence) that he believes cynics are just discouraged and closeted romantics who lack or have lost the courage of their underlying idealism.

At any rate, it's unlikely that real cynics have made it this far in this volume or this chapter—unless they're searching for the promised allusion to sex. It's coming. I would simply conclude by noting that the fact that Appreciative Inquiry is currently hot in the OD world need not be either a curse or a blessing as it is adapted and applied in evaluation. It will be judged on its merits according to the diverse criteria that evaluators bring to such judgments. From a utilization-focused perspective, it looks promising as yet another option available for certain primary intended users in those situations described in this volume.

I opened by quoting Sartre's observation that *words are loaded pistols.* Having opened with a violent reference, I promised to close with sex so as to give appreciative obeisance to these twin pillars of American society. The sex part comes not from me but from Ernie House, who has written a novel called *Where the Truth Lies,* about evaluation in the Big Apple, that includes some hot sex—well, sex anyway. This is no doubt part of Ernie's commitment to attract newcomers to our glamorous and underappreciated profession. It's a good read. You can undertake your own appreciative inquiry at http://house.ed.asu.edu. There's lots of intrigue but no violence—unless you consider data corruption, misinterpretation, and misuse forms of violence— I confess, I do.

Note

I want to offer a genuine appreciation, acknowledging not only my own gratitude but, if I may be so bold, that of the entire evaluation profession. This milestone one-hundredth volume of New Directions for Evaluation marks completion of the stellar edi-

Table 7.2. Corresponding Principles and Premises

Appreciative Inquiry	Utilization-Focused Evaluation
Constructivist AI Principle: The notion that multiple realities exist based on perceptions and shared understandings . . . suggests that what is known about an organization and the organization's actual destiny are interwoven.	U-FE Consequences Premise: What is perceived as real is real in its consequences (The Thomas Theorem*). Utility is in the eye of the user.
AI Principle of Simultaneity: Because reality is an evolving social construction, it is possible through inquiry to influence the reality an organization creates for itself. Inquiry and change are simultaneous and "inquiry is intervention."	U-FE Process Use: Going through the process of an evaluation can change those who experience the process as they learn to think evaluatively.
Poetic Principle: Because reality is a human construction, an organization is like an open book in which its story is being coauthored continually by its members and those who interact with them. Consequently, members are free to choose which part of the story to study or inquire about—its problems and needs or its moments of creativity or joy, or both.	Intended Use by Intended Users: Those who are the primary intended users of an evaluation determine its focus, its priorities, its primary purposes and uses—in short, they determine the evaluation story line based on intended use.
Anticipatory Principle: The image an organization has of its future guides that organization's current behavior. Thus, an organization's positive images of its future will anticipate, or lead to, positive actions.	The Necessity of Focus Premise: We cannot look at everything. What we focus on makes a difference to what we learn, think, and do. Focusing on evaluation use increases the likelihood of use.
Positive Principle: Early Appreciative Inquiry practitioners found that the more positive the questions they asked were, the more engaged and excited participants were and the more successful and longer lasting the change effort was. This is in large part because human beings and organizations want to turn toward positive images that give them energy and nourish happiness.	Engagement and Ownership: Intended users are more likely to use an evaluation if they feel positive about the evaluation's utility; they are more likely to feel positive if they understand and feel ownership of the evaluation process and findings; they are more likely to understand and feel ownership if they have been actively involved; by actively involving primary intended users, the evaluator is training users in use, preparing the groundwork for a positive approach to use, and reinforcing the intended utility of the evaluation every step along the way.

Note: The material in column 1 is from Chapter One of this volume.

*The Thomas Theorem suggests that a situation defined as real is real in its consequences.

torial partnership of Jennifer Greene and Gary Henry. They have been rigorous, bold, forward-looking, nurturing of new authors, and demanding of old-timers. They have nursed hundreds of drivel-filled manuscripts to evaluation brilliance—or at least adequacy. On behalf of the authors of this volume and the hundreds of authors and editors who have worked with Jennifer and Gary, we extend our deepest appreciation.

References

Brandl, J. "The Real Uses of Evaluation in the World of Politics." Address to the American Evaluation Association meeting, New Orleans, 1988.

Golembiewski, B. "Three Perspectives on Appreciative Inquiry." *OD Practitioner*, 2000, 32(1), 53–58.

Hopson, R. (ed.). *How and Why Language Matters in Evaluation.* New Directions for Evaluation, no. 86. San Francisco: Jossey-Bass, 2000.

Joint Committee on Standards for Educational Evaluation. *The Standards for Program Evaluation.* Thousand Oaks, Calif.: Sage, 1994.

Jones, L. "To Please or Not to Please." *Skeptical Briefs*, Mar. 2003, p. 12.

Kretzmann, J., and McKnight, J. *Building Communities from the Inside Out: A Path Toward Finding and Mobilizing Community Assets.* Chicago: Institute for Policy Research, Northwestern University, 1997.

Leffert, N., and others. "Developmental Assets: Measurement and Prediction of Risk Among Adolescents." *Applied Developmental Science*, 1998, 2(4), 209–230.

Mattessich, P., and Monsey, B. *Community Building: What Makes It Work: A Review of Factors Influencing Successful Community Building.* St. Paul, Minn.: Wilder Foundation, 1997.

Patton, M. Q. *Creative Evaluation.* (2nd ed.) Thousand Oaks, Calif.: Sage, 1987.

Patton, M. Q. *Utilization-Focused Evaluation.* (3rd ed.) Thousand Oaks, Calif.: Sage, 1997.

Patton, M. Q. "Organizational Development and Evaluation." *Canadian Journal of Evaluation*, 1999, special issue, 93–113.

Patton, M. Q. "Language Matters." In R. Hopson (ed.), *How and Why Language Matters in Evaluation.* New Directions for Evaluation, no. 86. San Francisco: Jossey-Bass, 2000.

Patton, M. Q. "Feminist, Yes, But Is It Evaluation?" In D. Seigart and S. Brisolara (eds.), *Feminist Evaluation: Explorations and Experiences.* New Directions for Evaluation, no. 96. San Francisco: Jossey-Bass, 2002.

Preskill, H., and Torres, R. T. *Evaluative Inquiry for Learning in Organizations.* Thousand Oaks, Calif.: Sage, 1999.

Rallis, S., and Rossman, G. "Dialogue for Learning: Evaluator as Critical Friend." In R. Hopson (ed.), *How and Why Language Matters in Evaluation.* New Directions for Evaluation, no. 86. San Francisco: Jossey-Bass, 2000.

Sorensen, P. F., Yaeger, T. F., and Nicoll, D. "Appreciative Inquiry: Fad or Important Focus for OD?" *OD Practitioner*, 2000, *32*, 1–5.

Torres, R. T., and Preskill, H. "Evaluation and Organizational Learning: Past, Present, and Future." *American Journal of Evaluation*, 2001, 22(3), 387–396.

Watkins, J. M., and Cooperrider, D. "Appreciative Inquiry: A Transformative Paradigm." *OD Practitioner*, 2000, *32*, 6–12.

Wineburg, S. "The Self-Fulfillment of the Self-Fulfilling Prophecy." *Educational Researcher*, Dec. 1987, pp. 28–37.

MICHAEL QUINN PATTON is a faculty member at the Union Institute and University.

INDEX

Back Issue/Subscription Order Form

Copy or detach and send to:
Jossey-Bass, A Wiley Company, 989 Market Street, San Francisco CA 94103-1741

Call or fax toll-free: Phone 888-378-2537 6:30AM – 3PM PST; Fax 888-481-2665

Back Issues: Please send me the following issues at $27 each
(Important: please include series abbreviation and issue number.
For example EV93)

_____

_____

_____

$ _____   Total for single issues

$ _____   SHIPPING CHARGES: SURFACE   Domestic Canadian
                                       First Item $5.00 $6.00
                                       Each Add'l Item $3.00 $1.50
               For next-day and second-day delivery rates, call the number listed above.

Subscriptions   Please __start __renew my subscription to *New Directions for
                Evaluation* for the year 2____at the following rate:

U.S.	__Individual $80	__Institutional $175
Canada	__Individual $80	__Institutional $215
All Others	__Individual $104	__Institutional $249
Online Subscription		__Institutional $193

**For more information about online subscriptions visit
www.interscience.wiley.com**

$ _____   Total single issues and subscriptions (Add appropriate sales tax
               for your state for single issue orders. No sales tax for U.S.
               subscriptions. Canadian residents, add GST for subscriptions and
               single issues.)

__Payment enclosed (U.S. check or money order only)
__VISA __MC __ AmEx # _____ Exp. Date _____

Signature _____ Day Phone _____
__ Bill Me (U.S. institutional orders only. Purchase order required.)

Purchase order # _____
                 Federal Tax ID13559302   **GST 89102 8052**

Name _____

Address _____

_____

Phone _____ E-mail _____

For more information about Jossey-Bass, visit our Web site at www.josseybass.com

OTHER TITLES AVAILABLE IN THE
NEW DIRECTIONS FOR EVALUATION SERIES
Jennifer C. Greene, Gary T. Henry, Coeditors-in-Chief

NEW DIRECTIONS FOR EVALUATION
IS NOW AVAILABLE ONLINE AT WILEY INTERSCIENCE

What is Wiley InterScience?

Wiley InterScience is the dynamic online content service from John Wiley & Sons delivering the full text of over 300 leading scientific, technical, medical, and professional journals, plus major reference works, the acclaimed Current Protocols laboratory manuals, and even the full text of select Wiley print books online.

What are some special features of Wiley InterScience?

Wiley Interscience Alerts is a service that delivers table of contents via e-mail for any journal available on Wiley InterScience as soon as a new issue is published online.
Early View is Wiley's exclusive service presenting individual articles online as soon as they are ready, even before the release of the compiled print issue. These articles are complete, peer-reviewed, and citable.
CrossRef is the innovative multi-publisher reference linking system enabling readers to move seamlessly from a reference in a journal article to the cited publication, typically located on a different server and published by a different publisher.

How can I access Wiley InterScience?

Visit http://www.interscience.wiley.com.

Guest Users can browse Wiley InterScience for unrestricted access to journal Tables of Contents and Article Abstracts, or use the powerful search engine.
Registered Users are provided with a *Personal Home Page* to store and manage customized alerts, searches, and links to favorite journals and articles. Additionally, Registered Users can view free Online Sample Issues and preview selected material from major reference works.
Licensed Customers are entitled to access full-text journal articles in PDF, with select journals also offering full-text HTML.

How do I become an Authorized User?

Authorized Users are individuals authorized by a paying Customer to have access to the journals in Wiley InterScience. For example, a University that subscribes to Wiley journals is considered to be the Customer.
Faculty, staff and students authorized by the University to have access to those journals in Wiley InterScience are Authorized Users. Users should contact their Library for information on which Wiley journals they have access to in Wiley InterScience.

ASK YOUR INSTITUTION ABOUT WILEY INTERSCIENCE TODAY!

Do they have the answers?

"Youth are a hidden resource to our society—they are creative and provide time, energy, and insight into the development of new ideas, community innovation, and volunteerism. More than ever, we need to make our youth true partners. They have to become part of the solution of the significant issues that face our times. *New Directions for Youth Development* is dedicated to helping this process through knowledge, experimentation in practice, and large-scale efforts to change our thinking and policies."

—GIL NOAM
   Harvard Graduate School of Education and McLean Hospital
   Editor-in-Chief

Personal Rate Subscriptions: $75 USD
Additional postage may apply for international subscribers.
Visit us at www.josseybass.com/go/ndyd